Compassion and Respect

*Breaking through to Dialogue on Abortion,
Family Planning and Human Reproduction
in a Secular, Pluralistic World*

JOHN J. MAWHINNEY

WIPF & STOCK · Eugene, Oregon

COMPASSION AND RESPECT
Breaking through to Dialogue on Abortion, Family Planning and Human Reproduction in a Secular, Pluralistic World

Copyright © 2020 John J. Mawhinney. All rights reserved. Except for brief quotations in critical publications or reviews, no part of this book may be reproduced in any manner without prior written permission from the publisher. Write: Permissions, Wipf and Stock Publishers, 199 W. 8th Ave., Suite 3, Eugene, OR 97401.

Wipf & Stock
An Imprint of Wipf and Stock Publishers
199 W. 8th Ave., Suite 3
Eugene, OR 97401

www.wipfandstock.com

PAPERBACK ISBN: 978-1-7252-7802-8
HARDCOVER ISBN: 978-1-7252-7803-5
EBOOK ISBN: 978-1-7252-7804-2

Manufactured in the U.S.A. OCTOBER 8, 2020

Scripture quotations are from New Revised Standard Version Bible, copyright © 1989 National Council of the Churches of Christ in the United States of America. Used by permission. All rights reserved worldwide.

Compassion and Respect

To my sisters, Mary Ann and Ellen,
To my niece, Mary Ellen Lynch Commiso
and her sons, Adrian and Sean,
To my nephew Thomas J. Lynch and his daughter,
Victoria Ann, and
To my nephew Dennis Lynch and his sons,
Aiden, Jude, and Nicholas

Contents

Acknowledgements | ix

Chapter 1: Overview and Perspectives | 1
A. Intended Audience
B. The Book's Perspective, Thrust, and Objective
C. Author's Resume, Academic Specialty, and Experience
D. Author's Methodology: What Is Societal Structural Justice Analysis?
E. Chapter Outlines

Chapter 2: Author's Ethical Model and the Time/Space Character of Human Existence | 12
A. The Author's Ethical Model
B. The Contextual Nature of All Human Knowledge: Ethical Implications

Chapter 3: Three Ancient Hebrew Stories of Origins | 26
A. Introduction
B. First Creation Story of Origins (Gen 1.:1—2:3)
C. Second Creation Story (Gen 2:4–24)
D. Third Story of Origins: The Rise of Evil and the Collapse and Disintegration of Harmony (Gen 3:1–24)

Chapter 4: Jesus, a Person for and with Others: Four Stories from the Gospel of Luke | 40
A. Introduction: How the Gospels Came to Be
B. A Roman Centurion Sends for Jesus (Luke 7:1–10)
C. Parable of the Good Samaritan (Luke 10:25–37)
D. Parable of the Prodigal Love of a Father for His Two Sons (Luke 15:11–32)
E. A Sinful Woman Loves and Is Forgiven; the Riddle/Parable of the Two Debtors (Luke 7:36–50)

Chapter 5: Compassion and Respect: Abortion Issues, Part One of Two | 56
A. Abortion: A Divisive, Intractable Issue
B. Dworkin: Overcoming Divisiveness by Finding a Mediating Middle Ground for Beginning Policy Discussion
C. The Official Roman Catholic Position on Abortion
D. Abortion and Compassion: Two Real-life Case Studies, Gustafson and Kaveny
E. Abortion: Legal Observations: Catherine Kaveny, Ronald Dworkin, and George Dennis O'Brien.

Chapter 6: Compassion and Respect: Abortion Issues, Part Two of Two | 78
A. Introduction: Morality of Abortion, Dworkin's Goal
B. The Unique Sacredness of All Human Life
C. Dworkin's Position on the Morality of Abortion. For Clarity of Exposition We Present Dworkin's Position in Three Units
D. Real-life Examples of Handicapped Children Who Have Coped

Chapter 7: Family Planning, Personhood, and Human Reproduction (IVF) | 95
A. The Importance of Family Planning and Contraception for Avoiding Unwanted Pregnancies
B. Personhood, Human Individuality, and Embryology Science
C. Human Reproduction: In-Vitro Fertilization (IVF)

Chapter 8: Public Policy Discourse: A Real-life Example | 112
A. Introduction
B. How the Issue Came Before the US Supreme Court
C. The Supreme Court Ruling as Public Policy Discourse
D. The Supreme Court Ruling as Societal Justice Analysis
E. The Court's Ruling as Searching for a Mediating Middle Ground
F. The Court's Decision as a Compassionate, Respectful Search for and Finding a Nonjudgmental Mediating Middle Ground
G. The Importance of Married Love for Society and Individuals
H. The Court's Decision as Compassionate, Respectful, and Nonjudgmental Interpretation of Law

Bibliography | 125
Index | 131

Acknowledgements

IT WAS THE LATE Jesuit, John C. Haughty, author of nine scholarly books on theology, who, after reading early drafts of its first two chapters, first urged the author to expand his manuscript and publish it.

Second, the author thanks the following for highly recommending his finished manuscript to Wipf and Stock Publishers: John L. Esposito, PhD, University Professor at Georgetown University and founder/director of the Prince Alwaleed Bin Talal Center for Muslim-Christian Understanding; Shane P. Martin, PhD, Provost, Seattle University; Mel P. Daly, MD, AGSF, CMI, Associate Professor of Medicine, Johns Hopkins School of Medicine and medical director of Gilchrist Hospice Center, Towson MD; Stephen C. Rowntree, SJ, PhD, Associate Professor Emeritus of Philosophy, Loyola University (New Orleans); and Jaime E. Robledo, PSS, STD, past rector and president of Assumption College and Seminary, San Antonio, TX.

The author also thanks the highly regarded Jesuit Scripture scholar, John R. Donahue, PhD, for carefully reviewing chapters 3 and 4 and for recommending to him Wipf and Stock Publishers.

Finally, the author is grateful to Jesuits George B. Wilson, STD, and James A. O'Brien, PhD (philosophy), for feedback on several chapters.

Acknowledgements

The author also thanks Mr. Thomas Raszewski, MLS, MA, director of the Knott Library of Saint Mary Seminary and University, Baltimore, MD, for generous research assistance.

Finally, and very importantly, the author thanks the editorial staff of Wipf and Stock: Matt Wimer, :Caleb Shupe, Ian Creeger, Zechariah Mickel,. They were very pleasant to work with and helpful with their excellent suggestions.

CHAPTER 1

Overview and Perspectives

THIS CHAPTER GIVES AN overview of the book and its author. It has five sections, A through E:

A. Intended Audience

B. The Book's Perspective, Thrust, and Objective

C. Author's Resume: Academic Specialty and Experience

D. Author's Methodology: What Is Societal Justice Analysis?

E. Chapter Outlines

A. Intended Audience

This book is written for all persons of good will, regardless of their faith or non-faith. By persons of good will we mean persons who feel driven and are committed, at least in some degree, to living responsible lives both for their own good and for that of others. Such persons desire to contribute to a more just, more peaceful, less conflictive and divided world, especially as it affects the marginalized and looked-down-upon and the emotionally or economically distressed.

How one thinks or speaks of what drives them to do so is not important. Some speak of it as personal God; others as simply some mysterious force. But whatever it is, they experience this force as awesome and as existentially and inescapably real as a sunset and bodily pain. They also find it an essential help for dealing with life's challenges. (We develop this point further in chapter 2, section A, when we explain our ethical model.)

This book does not assume that the reader has ever studied ethics, religion, or other specific academic discipline. Although based on much scholarship, the author writes, not in the language of scholars, but in a simple, straightforward language; hopefully accessible to any reader with some interest in abortion, family planning, contraception, LGBTQ, and human reproduction as public policy issues.

The book is also written in a way that allows readers to choose the chapters they wish to read and in what order. For example, some readers may not be interested in chapters 3 and 4 that approach the topic from a Hebrew/Christian scriptural angle.

The author sees himself, not so much as a scholar, but as an intellectual communicator. He likes to take quite complex, abstract ideas of scholars and "translate" them (without compromising their nuances) into a "language" that enables readers of all backgrounds to grasp and apply them to real-life, existential situations. As far as possible he avoids technical terms. When this is unavoidable, he immediately explains the term in a simpler language and usually with a concrete, real-life example.

The book may also be of interest to professionals who have occasion to counsel people on abortion and family planning and need to articulate their counsel in a simple, straightforward language, accessible even to those with a limited education. These professionals would include marriage counselors, physicians (especially gynecologists and obstetricians), psychologists, religious ministers of various faiths, and, perhaps, even politicians who may find parts of the book helpful for articulating their positions on politically and ethically sensitive issues, especially that of abortion.

Finally, the book is relevant for college liberal arts courses in public social policy, sociology, political science, and ethics (philosophical or religious).

B. Book's Perspective, Thrust, and Objective

Compassion, respect, understanding, readiness to forgive, responsibility, and accountability are virtues urgently needed in our global but acrimoniously divided world, including the United States. We now travel rapidly around the globe and electronically communicate with one another instantaneously, but this communication "*with*" is often not "*for*" one another but "*against*" one another. Increasingly vicious terrorist and hate groups of many stripes are pitting nations against one another as well as dividing their own citizenry from one another.

The book's primary objective and thrust is to foster respectful public dialogue on divisive public policy issues, especially abortion. Or, to put it in another way, our interest is to help people break through their differences enough to dialogue with one another. To this end, it seeks to provide ideas and a language that may be useful to those who wish to discuss divisive social issues in a public forum with others, whether they be small groups or a political audience.

Thus, our purpose is not to tell others what is morally right or wrong, but to get people to think more clearly and deeply about the issues we discuss and to respectfully learn from and collaborate with one another to make for a more peaceful, just world.

To carry on such dialogue, we need to recognize that we have no choice but to live in a secular, pluralistic world. (We explain how we understand the words "secular" and "pluralistic" in the next chapter.) This means that today, perhaps more than ever before, even those of us who live in the same community often have very different values and religious or religious-like convictions and so see life and its meaning in ways that often sharply conflict with those of others whom we must constantly rub shoulders with.

If this dialogue is to make headway, it is essential that people be ready to listen respectfully and nonjudgmentally to one another and try to understand where others are coming from. This does not require that we give up our own values and convictions, but it does mean a willingness to avoid advocating public policies that try to force others, especially by enacting laws, to act against their good-faith consciences. Instead, we need to search for pragmatic, workable public policy compromises and accommodations that all can live with even though no one will be fully satisfied.

From the US perspective, uncompromising acrimony tears apart the social fabric on which our nation was built. Our Founding Fathers prided themselves on respecting the freedom of expression and strongly held personal and religious convictions and practices of others.

The rather rapid ratification of the US Constitution by all thirteen colonies was possible only because our Founding Fathers were able to find ways to accommodate deep political, religious, and even ethical differences among themselves by finding "mediating middle ground" compromises and accommodations.

Politically, they created a Congress with two legislative bodies: a Senate, where every state has an equal representation regardless of population size and, to accommodate states with large numbers of citizens, a House of Representatives, where each state has a representation based on the number of citizens it has. To elect the nation's president and vice president, they created an Electoral College, where each state has a number of

Overview and Perspectives

representatives equal to the number of representatives and senators it has in Congress. After the thirteen colonies approved the Constitution the passed amendments that guaranteed freedom of religion and speech.

For this reason, among others, the author of this book does not think it too much to ask of one another to look for mediating middle-ground compromises over the acrimonious issue of abortion and the other issues discussed.

Since our objective is to foster respectful and understanding dialogue, we do not formally take ethical positions on the issues discussed. Some say all dialogue on such issues, especially on abortion and LGBTQ, is impossible because the various sides are too acrimoniously locked into their positions. However, we do not accept this pessimistic view.

C. Author's Resume, Academic Specialty, and Experience

The author is a professional ethicist. He earned his PhD from the Religion department of Temple University (a Pennsylvania's State university), specializing in societal structural justice analysis (to be explained a couple of pages below). Later, to better understand the business mentality and advise others, he obtained a MBA in the executive business program of Loyola University, Baltimore.

"Religiously" the author sees himself as a secularly religious, pluralist, ecumenical Christian and socially committed humanist. He believes that one's faith is not manifested by the doctrines one claims to believe in or by the rituals one practices, but by how one lives out one's life.[1] The author explains

---

1. According to a Catholic priest friend, this is how Pope Francis speaks of true faith. It is also the way Karen Armstrong speaks of religious faith in her books, *A History of God: The 4,000 Year Quest of Judaism, Christianity,* and *Islam* (1994); *The Case for God: What Religion Really Means* (2009), and *Twelve Steps to a Compassionate Life* (2011).

what he means by "secular" and "religious" at the beginning of chapter 2.

After receiving his doctorate, he was appointed acting associate dean of the Evening School and of societal justice programs at Loyola University (Baltimore).

After leaving Loyola (Baltimore) in 1979, he had the opportunity to refine his understanding and method of societal structural justice analysis during an eleven-year period (1979–90) when he was asked to develop a special program under the sociology department of the Loyola University in New Orleans. The objective of the program was to awaken his own as well as his students' awareness of the societal ethical dimensions and dilemmas posed by US foreign (political, economic, and military) policies. The focus was primarily on Central America. He also taught special tutorials in ethics.

For five years during this period the author was also associate director of the University's Institute of Human Relations; his responsibilities included writing and editing monthly articles for the university's publication, *Blueprint for Social Justice*.

In 1990, he had the opportunity to go to Central America where he worked for ten years (1990–99). There, in collaboration with a Salvadoran agronomist, he developed economic projects to help very poor Salvadoran peasant farmers (known as *campesinos*). His role was to write up and negotiate grant proposals for projects that might economically benefit poor subsistent farmers. (The author is fluent in reading, writing, and speaking Spanish.) The projects came through a Salvadoran government agency that was funded by the United States.

His Salvadoran collaborator designed the technical aspects of the projects and oversaw their execution. To make the projects more effective, he and his agronomist collaborator developed an effective working relationship with the very progressive mayor of the tiny, rural town where they implemented most of their projects.

In this connection the author wrote and published a popular booklet aimed at very poor, barely literate, rural *campesinos* on how to do organic agriculture. He wrote the text based on what he had learned from his Salvadoran collaborator; a Salvadoran nonprofit organization that specialized in popular education for the very poor, and drew cartoons to accompany the text.

Since returning to the United States in 1999, the author has involved himself in fundraising for and giving economic and other counseling to low income friends he had made in El Salvador.

D. Author's Methodology: What is Societal Structural Justice Analysis?

Societal structural justice analysis is multidisciplinary with important social science perspectives. Put simply, it is a method for uncovering our hidden, taken-for-granted, assumptions and attitudes that shape, underlie, and support the institutions of our society and make our institutions only more or less just, compassionate, and understanding of others, whether the others be individuals, small societal groupings, larger societies, or nations. To do such analysis, the author makes use of not only ethical and religious ideas but also those of sociology, political analysis, psychology, law, history, medicine, and other sciences. Some see societal structural justice analysis as risky work in that it can lead to a very radical criticism of the societies and institutions with which one identifies and to feelings of alienation, that is, of being pushed to the margins of these societies.

For some decades, the author focused his societal justice analysis primarily on US foreign policy (economic, political, and military). But after returning from Central America, he branched out to study some bioethical issues as well as US poverty and the increasingly widening income gap (in percentages, not just absolute terms) between middle class and highly wealthy Americans. In 2016 a Catholic professor of moral theology asked the author to team up with him to do research for several years on how to promote and engage in bioethical discourse in a secular, pluralistic world. This research gave the author the idea to write this book.

The development of the author's societal structural justice model was further enhanced by twenty years of collaboration with the Interfaith Center on Corporate Responsibility in New York City. In this work he dialogued with some top executives of major business corporations. He also presented from the floor of annual stockholders' meetings corporate social responsibility resolutions on behalf of various religious groups who held investment stock in these corporations.

The objective of all the author's ethical work has always been to contribute to a more tolerant, more understanding, more peaceful, more just world. Given our finitude and messy, nitty-gritty world, this requires us to come together with others to figure out what is not only ethically the more responsible, but also what is pragmatically achievable. The author sees his book as continuing, and perhaps culminating, his sixty some year commitment to the promotion of societal structural justice, especially for the marginalized and the poor.

E. Chapter Outlines

Chapter 1 discusses the audience the book is intended for and the perspective the author comes from. It includes the author's resume, academic specialty (societal justice analysis), and academic and other experience. The chapter also gives a brief statement of the contents of the book.

Chapter 2 explains each element in the author's responsible, secular, religious, compassionate, respectful model for doing ethics and the contextual character of all human knowledge and its truth value, including our understanding of ethical norms. The author employs this model in addressing the ethical issues discussed in the book's last four chapters.

Chapters 3 and 4 minutely examine seven stories from the Hebrew and Christian Scriptures. The author presents them only as "stories" because they are not analyzed for their Hebraic or Christian theological and faith messages, but for their secularly religious, ethical messages. They imaginatively and concretely highlight key notions of the author's model for doing ethics, much like *Sesame Street* stories highlight ethical behavior for children, except we do it for grownups. These notions include: the unique, "godlike," "sacred" character of humans, their "godlike" dominion over creation, their obligation to exercise this dominion responsibly and accountably, and the religious attitude or "temperament" one should have toward life and its meaningfulness. A well-known and highly published Jesuit Biblical scholar, John R. Donahue, checked the analyses and found them fully in accord with up-to-date Hebrew-Christian Biblical scholarship.

Chapter 5 makes use of Pewforum surveys to highlight our acrimonious divisiveness over the morality of abortion, including even among members of the same church. It next analyzes in detail the official Roman Catholic position on abortion, not to refute or defend it, but because it is the clearest and most nuanced statement of the pro-life position.

The author give a thorough presentation of of the Catholic position, of the renowned jurist and philosopher, Ronald Dworkin, for how we might overcome our divisiveness. (Dworkin's proposal is examined in much more detail in chapter 6.)

Then to help keep both his own and his reader's feet on the ground, the chapter analyzes at length two real-life case-studies on abortion, one by the well-known Protestant moral theologian, James M. Gustafson; the other by the highly respected Catholic theologian/lawyer, Cathleen Kaveny. These cases are very important for understanding the author's model for doing ethics and Dworkin's liberal position. The chapter ends with some legal observations on abortion made by Cathleen Kaveny, Ronald Dworkin, George Dennis O'Brien, and others.

However, Dworkin's position is not radically pro-choice, for he holds that every abortion is ethically problematic and tragic, though at times justifiable. The first major section of the chapter explains Dworkin's very nuanced understanding of the unique sacredness of all forms of human life. It then discusses how Dworkin sees the views of conservatives and liberals as ranging over a broad, quite nuanced spectrum.

Chapter 7 discusses family planning and contraception; why embryology, as a science, does not and cannot support the notion that an embryo or fetus is a person; and finally human reproduction procedures (in-vitro fertilization, or IVF) and some ethical issues they raise.

The concluding chapter 8 touches on LGBTQ issues by analyzing in considerable detail the 2015 Supreme Court ruling on same-sex marriage.[2] It explains how this ruling is a real-life example of public policy discourse, societal justice analysis, and how to search for a mediating middle ground when faced with seriously divisive ethical issues.

The narrow five-four ruling declared that all states must license same-sex marriages and recognize those performed in other states. It is also an example how to interprete law with compassion. Recall that in chapter 4 we called attention to Jesus' harsh criticisms of many teachers of the Mosaic law because their interpretations of the law were often lacking in compassion. This Supreme ruling is also a magnificent example of interpreting law compassionately.

---

2. LGBTQ. In this abbreviation, the letter "L" refers to lesbians; the letter "G" to gays; the letter "B" to those with sexual feelings for both their own sex and the opposite sex, the letter "T" to those with the genital of one sex but with sexual feelings of the other sex; and "Q" to those who question, that is, are unsure of what their sexual orientation is.

OVERVIEW AND PERSPECTIVES

In effect this book creates a number of mini-conversations or exchanges between Dworkiin and eight Protestant and Catholic Catholic theologians, philosophers, and lawyers of the last seventy years: Karen Armstrong. Lisa Solle Cahill, Margaret A. Farley, James M. Gustafson, Cathleen Kaveny, H. Richard Niebuhr, George Dennis O'Brien, and Charles Taylor.

CHAPTER 2

Author's Ethical Model and the Time/Space Character of Human Existence

THIS CHAPTER GIVES A thorough presentation of the author's model for doing ethics and the ethical implications of the fact that all human knowledge is contextual, that is, relative/relational to the historical (time/space/place) where one find oneself. It has two sections, A and B.

A. The Author's Ethical Model

B. The Contextual Nature of All Human Knowledge: Ethical Implications

A. The Author's Ethical Model[1]

The author's model for doing ethics is what he he speaks of as the responsible/accountable self model. It is built around four

---

1. The articulation of the author's ethical model goes back to the writings of H. Richard Niebuhr (1894–1962), not to be confused with his more famous brother, Reinhold. See Niebuhr, *Responsible Self*, 47–68.

 H. Richard Niebuhr was a highly respected twentieth-century Protestant theologian with a strong sociological bent; for example, see his books *Radical Monotheism and Western Culture*, *Christ and Culture*, and *The Social Sources of Denominationalism*. The author's dissertation focused on how H. Richard

notions: (1) ethical responsibility and accountability; (2) secularity and pluralism; (3) the religious attitude or temperament; and (4) the virtues of compassion and respect.

(1) *The model is ethically responsible and accountable.* Every self and societal grouping is responsible and accountable to oneself as well as to other selves and to one's own society and to the world one lives in. It recognizes: (a) that we humans are finite, limited beings; (b) that our choices are often not clear-cut and so are not black and white, for often we are faced with situations where the ethical choice is not between a good and an evil but only from among many evils or even from among many of the worst of the worst evils; and (c) that we humans live in a very dirty, messy, nitty-gritty world where we often have to make pragmatic, workable decisions that are not by any means morally ideal.

So, our model for doing ethics focuses on our duty to determine what is the more (and hopefully the most) responsible and accountable thing to do rather than on traditional "do and don't" models or "pursuit of the ideal good" models for doing ethics.[2]

(2) *The model is secular and pluralistic.* The author uses the words "secular" and "secularity" in opposition to the words "secularist" and "secularism."[3] He developed the distinction after reading Charles Taylor's *A Secular Age*.[4]

Niebuhr's way of thinking has a universalistic thrust in the sense that it reaches out, not just to Christians but also to nonbelievers of good will.

2. Philosophers speak of "do and don't" models for doing ethics as "deontological" (from the Greek word, *deon*, meaning "duty" or "obligation"). They speak of the pursuit of the ideal good models as "teleological" (from the Greek word, *telos*, meaning "end" or "goal"). We avoid these technical philosophical terms.

3. For a précis-like statement of his distinction, see Taylor's introductory chapter in *A Secular Age*, 1–22. Taylor is a well-respected Canadian Catholic philosopher. See also Berger, *Sacred*, 105–7. The three chapters on these pages develop Berger's understating of secularity.

4. Taylor, *Secular Age*.

Briefly, the words "*secularist*" and "*secularism*" were coined about 1850 to denote a system that sought to understand life *solely* on principles taken from this world and without recourse to any belief in a transcendent God or a future life.

In contrast, the words "secular" and "secularity," as Taylor and we use them, refer to a world where most people do not outright reject or feel hostile toward God and religion but rather find other, more satisfying options for dealing with the wonders, mysteries, challenges, and tragedies of life. Such people feel they can cope with life without thinking about spiritual matters in explicit, self-conscious, traditionally religious ways.

Today most people, including the traditionally religious, recognize and respect that there are a plurality of ways for understanding the world and life in it without having recourse to traditionally religious language, rituals, and other symbols. This does not mean (as we explain next in point 3) that persons may not be deeply religious in some other sense.

Also, today many people, especially in modern Western societies, regard religion or its absence as largely a private matter. For this reason, many no longer self-identify with some organized form of religion or, if they do, engage little in its rituals and often disregard many of its teachings.

Like it or not, the fact that we have been born into a secular, pluralistic world means that even traditionally religious people daily and unavoidably rub elbows with people with a wide variety of ways of looking at life. So, they have no choice but to find ways to get along with those who are not traditionally religious. Doing so affects, in turn, even how the traditionally religious see the world and life in it. Thus, secularity impacts everyone, whether they are believers in a personal God or nonbelievers.

In his lengthy book, Taylor traces in minute detail the gradual, largely imperceptible evolution of modern secular, pluralistic Western worldviews. He shows how the modern Western worldview gradually evolved and, to a large extent, displaced the once dominant and essentially monist (i.e., a basically unitary, generally accepted), largely Western Medieval and early Modern Christian worldviews. As a result of this evolution and its widespread reach, even most traditionally religious people today have become more or less comfortable with living in a secular, pluralistic world.

(3) *The model is religious.* It focuses on what one might call the religious or spiritual attitude or temperament. For many this attitude is more significant than the traditional notion of "religious belongingness," that is, the practice of self-identifying with some more or less traditionally organized form of religion. Ronald Dworkin explains the religious attitude in his Einstein Lectures, *Religion without God*.[5]

The religious or spiritual attitude rests on the recognition that everyone, willy-nilly, experiences some inexplicable, ineffable, mysterious "force" in the depth of one's "beingness." This force, though emotionally felt, is as truly and inescapably real as the experience of seeing a sunset or feeling bodily pain. We don't, and cannot, discover this force by "reason"; rather, to repeat, we experience it and know its reality just as we experience a sunset or bodily pain.[6]

---

5. Dworkin gave his Einstein Lectures in 2012, the year before his death. They are the best explanation of what he (and we) mean by the religious or spiritual attitude or temperament. Dworkin was an American philosopher, jurist, and scholar of US constitutional law. He was Frank Henry Sommer Professor of Law and Philosophy at New York University and Professor of Jurisprudence at University College, London. He also had taught at Oxford University and Yale Law School. Like Dworkin, Einstein saw himself as deeply religious even though he had no belief in some kind of "god."

Our articulation of the religious or spiritual attitude or temperament here is based on Dworkin. It is equally well articulated, from a different angle, by Karen Armstrong. See her *Case for God*, ix–xviii, 2–26, and 318–30.

6. Dworkin rightly holds that one cannot "prove" the existence of this mysterious force by any "rational" argument, such as many philosophers and theologians have tried for centuries to prove the existence of a personal God.

Dworkin's point is that true ethical/moral judgments for living an ethical or moral life are not just expressions of emotions.[7]

The experience of this mysterious force, call it what you will, never goes away; it is inescapable, though some seem to manage to ignore it by closing themselves up, as it were, in some kind of self-created, windowless, impenetrable, and sound-proof structure. Dworkin's understanding of this force might be called a secular form of god-talk.

This force urges the self to make responsible, accountable, and constructive commitments and to actively engage oneself in contributing to a better, more compassionate world, no matter how tiny be the cranny or niche of the world where this self happens to find itself and must work from. Given the size of the cosmos and its history, this niche is comparatively so infinitesimally small that it is no bigger than the size of the "period" that ends this sentence. The reality of this force also enables us to cope with life's difficulties and horrors.

(4) *The model is compassionate and respectful.*[8] Excellent illustrations of what we mean by these two words are found in the Hebrew and Christian Scriptures. (See our analyses in chapters 3 and 4 of three Hebrew and four Christian biblical stories that imaginatively portray God and Jesus as compassionate, understanding, and forgiving.)

Compassionate and respectful persons reach out to others and, at least to some extent, genuinely feel their pain, especially in in the case of the physically, emotionally, and economically needy, the suffering, and the outcast. Because they have such feelings, they pour out a healing care, a confirming presence. They want and actively try to do all in their power to ease the pain of others.

---

7. A philosopher might speak of the reality of this force as metaphysically or ontologically grounded or existentially real.

8. For Biblical views of compassion, see Adam, "Compassion," 157–59.

Author's Ethical Model

In return, persons who experience the compassion of another feel they have been genuinely listened to with an opened mind and with loving kindness. The fact that they have "been listened to" gives them a sense of peace, thanksgiving, more self-respect and self-esteem, and a desire to praise that other. If they have wronged another or society at large, those who have experienced the compassion of another feel a sense of forgiveness and understanding; they feel a welcoming re-acceptance back into a loving community.

Karen Armstrong (b. 1944): Compassion. In 2007 Armstrong won a $100,000 prize from the nonprofit Technology, Design, Entertainment (TDE) organization. Each year TDE gives a huge cash award to some individual who it thinks has made a difference and who, with their help, could make even a greater impact. Recipients can use their award any way they want. Armstrong immediately knew what she wanted. With her award, Armstrong established the website "Charter for Compassion," which sends out regular emails on this topic to all who sign up. Likewise, she has written a straightforward, thought-provoking book, *Twelve Steps to a Compassionate Life*. It sets out a program that can lead us toward a more compassionate life.[9] It suggests concrete ways we can enhance compassion and put compassion into action in everyday life by encouraging us to listen to one another's narratives. For Armstrong a

---

9. Armstrong, *Compassion*. See also her website: https://charterfocompasssion.org. She has published nearly thirty books. Her work has been translated into forty-five languages. She has addressed members of the U.S. Congress on three occasions; lectured to policy makers at the U.S. State Department; participated in the World Economic Forum in New York, Jordan, and Davos; addressed the Council on Foreign Relations in Washington and New York. She is increasingly invited to speak in Muslim countries and is now an ambassador for the UN Alliance of Civilizations. Her books have been praised in the *Washington Post, Christian Science Monitor, Financial Times,* and elsewhere. Though not strictly an academic, she has two honorary doctorates and her books prove that she is a scholar among the best of them on the history of world religions.

compassionate life is not just a matter of the heart or mind but a deliberate and often life-altering commingling of the two.

A chief task of our time, she wrote, must be to build a global community in which all peoples can live together in mutual respect. Yet, because of their dogmatism, religions, which should be making a major contribution to this end, are often part of the problem. All faiths recognize that compassion is the test of true spirituality and that it brings us into relation with absolutely transcendent mystery which we variously speak of as God, Brahman, Nirvana, Dao, etc. Every religion has formulated its own version of what is sometimes called the Golden Rule. In its most positive form, the rule states: "Always treat others as you wish to be treated yourself." (See the Christian "Our Father" prayer.) Further, the rule also insists that you cannot confine your benevolence to your own group; you must have concern for everybody, even your enemies.

She sees compassion as intrinsic to all human beings but each needs to work diligently to cultivate and expand their capacity for it. Sadly, she notes, we hear little about compassion these days.

More on Understanding Responsibility and Accountability. To do what is the most responsible and accountable thing, we need to keep in mind four points. First, every moral situation that we face calls for a "fitting" response.

Second, the response we make is always to our "interpretation" of the situation in which each self finds itself in space and time. So we must always ask ourselves if our interpretation of the other is adequately accurate. To answer this question we must carefully consider all that is going on, all that is driving our and others' interpretations of the situation, and all the values and disvalues, options, and non-options that may be involved.

Third, the other's response to us will be an interpretation of our response. So, in responding we must be careful that the other does not misinterpret what we say or do. That is why diplomatic, peace, and trade negotiations take so much time. Each side is not only trying to get the best it can for itself but also must spend lots of time just trying to find where the other is coming from and how to communicate clearly with that other.

Fourth, our responses almost always have a "societal" dimension that reaches beyond the people or groups that we are dialoguing with. So, its impacts usually extend well beyond themselves.

This is what a "responsible/accountable-self" model for doing ethics is all about. These four points are essential to keep in mind when engaging in the type of dialogue we promote in this book.

Pragmatic Truth. This author's thinking has also been influenced by the US philosopher/psychologist William James (1842–1910).[10] James saw truth as that which puts us in better relationship with the whole of reality. To find such "pragmatic" truth" (i.e., workable, effective, making a difference truth), he advocated a tough-minded empiricism that requires us to examine the real-life consequences of what we do or want to do. In other words, we are to respond to the flux of human life as it comes to us in concrete real-life situations. Because he saw "truth" in this way, he rejected "absolutely absolute" moral norms as too fixated to deal with many, perhaps most, real-life situations.

What do we mean by "absolutely absolute"? Traditional "do and don't" models for doing ethics focus on what one must do or not do. Examples are: thou shall not kill, thou shall not lie, and thou shall not steal. However, philosophers have always recognized that there are exceptions to do and don't commandments. For example, we can kill a person to prevent that person from killing another; a desperately poor person can steal some food to feed a hungry baby; one can lie to prevent another from

---

10. *James: Writings.* See sections on "Pragmatism," The "Pluralistic Universe," and "The Meaning of Truth.

killing her mother; and in a justifiable war, one can kill one's enemy. Of course, societies should have laws that make such exceptions as rare and as unnecessary as possible, such as having police forces to patrol our streets and welfare programs and governmental and privately funded food kitchens to aid the poor and homeless. But often these services are not enough.

The pursuit of the "ideal good" model is also important. All humans feel an urge and need to have some moral ideals if they are to live a moral life. In that limited sense, these models are absolute.

Both models serve well for most day-to-day life. However, they are not useful for all the moral challenges we the word 'face; so they are not "absolutely absolute." For, it is often not clear what one should morally and ideally do or strive for. It was for this reason that H. Richard Niebuhr proposed his "responsible/accountable self" model for doing ethics. We strive for and do what is realistically possible. In other words, we do the best we can.

B. The Contextual Nature of All Human Knowledge: Ethical Implications[11]

Because we humans are finite, space/time bound, and limited, all human knowledge and truth are at best only partial, that is, contextual and relative/relational to the history (time, space, place) that has formed us as well as to the time/place we presently live in. We know absolute, infinite mystery only analogously, relatively, and very inadequately.[12] We grasp the infinite, and even the finite, only in very limited ways.

---

11. This section deals with what philosophers call epistemology and what sociology theorists call the sociology of knowledge. We do not employ these terms here because even many well-educated people find them abstruse.

12. In the long historical, Christian scholastic tradition, theologians held that every statement made about God or infinite Mystery had to be immediately negated because it is, at best only analogously true, that is, only somewhat

Author's Ethical Model

This is true not only for today but throughout the history of religions. In her book, *A History of God*, and other writings Karen Armstrong makes this point very well.[13] The word "God" is only "a symbol of a reality that ineffably transcends us finite beings. God is not "being"; God is timeless and placeless mystery and beyond all being. And today more and more people are finding that the word "god" no longer works well for them. In our secular, pluralistic world, many need to and do think about life, its wonders, and its tragedies in ways very different from traditional religion.

Truth and Scientific Predictive Theory. Though our major interest is in the question of knowledge and its truth value in ethics, we first speak of the relative/relational value of scientific knowledge and truth value as understood by modern scientists. The only method that modern empirical scientists make use of is often spoken of as "predictive" theory.

First, scientists evaluate the truth value of a theory in two ways. First, the theory must give a coherent explanation of the scientific data thus far discovered and also be verifiable, at least to some degree, by allowing scientists to find confirmation of the theory through scientific observations or experiments.

However, second, it is not enough for a scientific theory to be just empirically verifiable and able to explain the data already found. The theory must also help scientists to discover more scientific data by leading them either to make new experiments and observations that they had not previously thought to make or look for. As new scientific data is found through new experiments or observations, the most imaginative scientists develop new, more comprehensive, and more satisfactory theories to explain the additional data that they have discovered.

---

true or only finitely and very inadequately true.

13. The subtitle of this book is: *The 4,000-Year Quest of Judaism, Christianity, and Islam*. For what we write here, see, for example, *History of God*, 177 and 196–97. Though not an academic, Armstrong (1944–present) is perhaps the greatest theologian of spirituality of the twentieth century.

This is how scientists advance their scientific knowledge. It is a step-by-step process. So, their search for "truth" never ends. And the "truth" scientists acquire is always contextual and relative/relational to the progress science has thus far made.

The Truth Value of Ethical (Moral) Knowledge. What is true for scientific knowledge also holds for ethical, societal-cultural mores and ethical/moral codes of conduct for two reasons. First, no ethical or moral norms or societal-cultural mores can foresee and account for every possible ethical situation and moral dilemma humans must deal with. Our finite world and our life in it are just too nitty-gritty for that. There is no such thing as a one-size-fits-all morality that fits every culture and situation.

For our societal-cultural situations are ever evolving. There are ever-new technological developments, systems of communication and surveillance, new political forms of governing, new ways of thinking about sex and marriage, new weapons of mass destruction (nuclear, biological, and chemical), and new missile delivery system (by drones, from space satellites, or from submarines deep in the ocean).[14] All this change is constantly posing new moral challenges.

So moral codes and societal-cultural mores continually evolve and must be updated to keep up with newly evolving situations. After all, the reason for developing moral codes and societal-cultural mores is to enable us to get along together, whether as individuals or as large or small societal groupings, including the world of nations. This is why we constantly update or make new international trade and peace agreements. That is why we must be realistic and pragmatic.

At best, we can formulate only some moral guidelines that we must always be ever-ready to modify or even put aside when

---

14. Our final chapter (8) gives a concrete example of how the thinking and insights of many have evolved in regards to married love and its profound meaning and impact not only for the married couple themselves but for society at large.

they no longer provide fitting, effective, workable, responsible, accountable solutions to the societal, structural, and cultural real-life situations that keep popping up. Think of the privacy issues that our electronic age is raising. Privacy is a value; but how are we to think about and deal with it in our reaL-life situations of today?

This is also true for our analysis of the ethical issues raised by contemporary advancements in medicine and human reproduction science. Today's scientists are also developing ever-new, compassionate technologies that offer new hope for people with family planning and other human reproduction challenges.

As we will discuss in chapter 4, Jesus strongly criticized the teachers of Mosaic law of his day for their overly rigid interpretations and applications of this law. Jesus saw these teachers as failing to incorporate into their interpretations the virtues of love, benevolence, respect, and understanding and so failed to be adequately loving, compassionate, and forgiving in addressing real-life situations. How can we incorporate these virtues when thinking about abortion, family planning, contraception, LGBTQ, and human reproduction? These issues we deal with in chapters 5–8.[15]

Applying ethical norms and mores in the messy, nitty-gritty situations of human life requires deep discernment of all aspects of a real-life situation. Moral discernment requires moral wisdom and, for us humans, this is very hard to come by.

Moral Discernment. This requires that we listen carefully, respectfully, and compassionately to people in their real-life predicaments. For example, it is certainly morally great when a person is willing to donate a kidney to save the life of another but it is not something one can morally demand. Also even a decision to donate a kidney needs to be discerned wisely. Most

---

15. Again, "L" refers to lesbians, "G" to gays, "B" to those with double sexual orientations, "T" to those with the genitals of one sex, but the feelings of another, and "Q" to those who question or are not sure of what their real sexual orientation.

would not consider it wise for a very young person to donate a kidney to an elderly person of eighty. A potential kidney donor should consider all aspects of her real-life situation as well as that of the would-be recipient.

We have historical proof that ethical norms and societal-cultural mores have always evolved. Some examples: we no longer think that some are born to be nobles and others to be serfs (or even worst, slaves); we no longer burn heretics at the stake in the hope that they will repent of their errors and save their souls; we no longer consider slavery ethically permissible; more and more of us no longer consider people of another race, ethnic group, or skin color to be inferior or better than those of another. Likewise, attitudes toward women and those with diverse sexual orientations have also been changing, though there is still much room and need for much more progress.

And the list could go on and on. However, in saying this, we are not suggesting moral evolution is always for the better.

Another way of speaking of relative/relational "truth" is to recall what we said about William James: a moral norm is true only insofar as it puts us in better relationships with the whole of reality and allows society to function more equitably and fairly. In other words, truth must be pragmatic and realistic and take in the whole real-life situation with all its dilemmas and hopes.

To be concrete about our point that our finite world is just too messy, nitty-gritty for a one-size-fits-all morality, consider the following real-life examples: (1) Consider prostitutes who economically can get through life only by selling their bodies; should this be called by the dirty name of prostitution or is it just a realistic effort to get through life?[16] (2) Take a desperately poor single-parent mother who, to get enough food for herself and her child (or children), cheats on food stamps and other welfare

---

16. We are not thinking here of "high-end" prostitutes who cater to the rich and powerful, but low-end ones who have to struggle just get by.

programs; (3) Think of those who have lost their job and home and cannot find another and so must live, often with children, on the streets or, if lucky, in a broken-down car and hope that they can get at least one meal a day at some soup kitchen or perhaps a few dollar handout to buy a bit to eat for their family. What societal mores do they need to develop to deal with their situation? (4) Take the same single-parent mother who has one or more boyfriends who give her a bit of money that help her feed her child or children as well as get a bit of sexual satisfaction that helps ease her difficult life. Again, this last situation should not be considered prostitution but a way of coping with a real-life existence.

These concrete examples are horrendous and, at least to some extent, destroy one's humanity and dignity both in one's own eyes and in the eyes of others. However, the examples do reflect real human existence in the dirty, messy, nitty-gritty world that all of us must deal with and do so with compassion.

What we argue here has implications for how we look at the morality of abortion as well as that of family planning, contraception, LGBTQ orientations, and the use of reproduction technologies such as in-vitro fertilization (IVF), though the last three are often less ethically contentious than abortion. (On this point see chapters 5–8.)

Attitudes and Mindsets. Finally, we need to keep in mind the variety of attitudes and mindsets that people have when dealing with life, ethical decision-making, and societal-cultural change. Some tend to be very conservative and traditional, others very progressive and liberal, and many in between. These mindsets, too, shape our ethical thinking and decision-making and how we are able to accept social change. They need to be taken into consideration in any societal justice analysis we engage it.

CHAPTER 3

Three Ancient Hebrew Stories of Origins[1]

THIS CHAPTER HIGHLIGHTS KEY ethical notions in the compassionate ethical model used in this book. We do so by analyzing the first three stories of the first book of the Hebrew Scriptures (Genesis 1–3). Our purpose is not to get the reader to religiously believe in them, but to imaginatively present our ethical notions. The chapter has four sections, A through D.

A. Introduction

B. First Creation Story of Origins (Gen 1:1—2:3)

C. Second Creation Story (Gen 2:4–24)

D. Third Story of Origins: The Rise of Evil and the Collapse and Disintegration of Harmony (Gen 3:1–24)

---

1. The well-known and well-published Jesuit Scripture scholar, John R. Donahue, reviewed this and the next chapter and found them in accord with up-to-date Scripture scholarship. He told me I could put him as a reference, PhD (University of Chicago in Ancient Near Eastern languages and civilizations), former holder of the Raymond E. Brown Chair of Scripture, St Mary's University, Baltimore, MD.

Three Ancient Hebrew Stories of Origins

A. Introduction[2]

The first book of the Hebrew Scriptures is called Genesis (meaning the origin, the coming to be of something). We deal only with the first three stories of Genesis (Gen 1:1—3:24). The oral traditions that gave rise to the stories go back many millennia. Undoubtedly during these millennia, the original oral traditions kept evolving considerably; so, we do not have the stories in their earliest form.

The first two stories (called creation stories) are about the origin, the coming to be of the cosmos as we have it today. The third story is not a creation story but a story of the origin of evil and the destruction of the original harmony and goodness of all God's creation.

Biblical scholars hold that the stories of Genesis were first written down after the fall of the Israelite monarchy around 586 BCE.[3] The Jews were then living in exile in Babylon. When writing them down, royal scribes revised and added to the earlier oral accounts because they wanted to reassure the Israelites, who were then living in exile, that their God, Yahweh, had not forgotten them but would bless them in the end, just as he had blessed their ancestors.

The two creation stories (Gen 1–2) give different accounts of how the Israelites conceptualized the coming-to-be of the cosmos as we have it today. Both stories assume that there had been a "preexisting something." Neither speaks of a "creation out of nothing" nor gives any explanation for how this "something came to be; it was just there.[4] God gave order to

---

2. Speiser, *Genesis*, liii-lviii, and notes and commentary on first three chapters, 3–13, 14–20, and 21–28.

3. In respect for other religions the abbreviations BCE (Before the Common BCE and CE (Common Era) are commonly used today instead of the abbreviations BC (Before Christ) and AD (anno Domini, Latin for "in the year of the Lord"). They refer to the same time periods.

4. Carr, *Genesis*, 11–13 (note 1:1—2:3). The notion of making something out of nothing did not develop until the first millennia BCE. There are only

this "something." The word "create" in this context has the sense of "making" or "bringing forth" something, just as an artisan brings forth or fashions a statue out of stone.[5]

Neither story suggests that God lived in some heavenly realm apart from the cosmos. The ancient Israelites and their neighboring peoples saw the cosmos as a single system or whole. There was no heavenly realm where the invisible gods and goddesses lived apart from humans nor was there a underworld where the invisible dead dwelt apart from the living.

The two stories differ in that the first story presents God as giving order to the cosmos day by day (though day is not to be understood as a twenty-four-hour day); the second portrays God as doing it in a step-by-step fashion, not a day by day one. Thus, both stories suggest some kind of evolutionary process.

B. First Creation Story of Origins (Gen 1:1—2:3)[6]

This story derives from the Jewish priestly tradition, which emphasized temple ritual. It dates to the Babylonian deportations of Jews in the early years of the sixth century BCE. Many

---

two references to the notion in the Bible. The first reference (2 Maccabees 7:28) is a very vague reference. Second Maccabees was written in Greek (not Hebrew) probably in Alexandria, Egypt about the first century BCE (after Judea had fallen under the control of the Syrian Seleucid Empire); it is not part of the canon of Jewish Scriptures. The second reference is Romans 4:17. This letter was written in Greek late in Paul's missionary life, between 52 to 58 CE—some years before any of the Gospels had been written. The Christian teaching that there was a creation out of nothing was not officially adopted until the Christian Council of Nicaea in 325.

5. See Hiebert, "Create, to," 770–71.

6. Speiser, *Genesis*, 3–13. The name used for God in the first creation story is the Hebrew word *eloah*, the generic Hebrew word for a divine being. (The plural of this word is used in the Hebrew Scriptures when referring to the many gods of other peoples.) This Hebrew word occurs only fifty-seven times and only in the portions of the Hebrew bible written in Aramaic. The second creation story refers to God as Yahweh, which is usually translated as "Lord God"; (in the Anchor Bible, it is translated as "God Yahweh"). See also Seow, "God, Names of," 588–95.

scholars think that it may have been originally meant as a preface to the second creation story. It presupposes the preexistence of the heavens and the earth" (Gen 1:1) and describes it as disordered, chaotic, empty, void and formless abyss that had wind sweeping over its waters (Gen 1:1–2). However, there is no effort to explain how this "preexisting" came to be; it was just there.

The story portrays God as issuing king-like decrees that give order to this chaotic abyss to make it the cosmos as we know it today.[7] He did so over a period of six days. (But the word "day" is not be taken literally as in our twenty-four-hour day.) This step-by-step, day by day ordering suggests an evolutionary process. But "evolutionary" is not to be understood in the way we think of scientific evolution today.

Thereby God transformed the chaotic, empty abyss into a viable habitat for all life. including humans. To further show his power, God, also king-like, gave names to all he brought bring forth. (Giving decrees and naming were prerogatives of only kings enjoyed.)

On day one, God decreed that the light be separated from the darkness, naming one "Night" and the other "Day." So, there was morning and evening. On the second day, he put a dome in the midst of the waters to separate the waters above the dome from the waters below the dome. He named the dome "Sky."

---

7. Modern astrophysicists believe that the cosmos, as we see it today, looks essentially the same as the one the ancients saw. They, too, believe it started with a preexisting something. For these scientists this something was originally no bigger than one-trillionth of the size of the period that ends this sentence. It contained all the space, matter, and energy but it was so hot that it had to burst. The bursting continues today and there is no telling whether it will ever stop doing so. This is known as the Big Bang Theory and is held by essentially every astrophysicist. They see no reason that it might be replaced by another theory in the foreseeable future. Scientists do not speculate on how this ball of energy came to be. For an excellent layperson's introduction, see Tyson, *Astrophysics*.

On the third, God gathered the waters below the dome into one place to let dry land appear. He called the dry land "Earth" and the waters "Seas." "And he "saw that it was good." On the third day, he also had the earth bring forth all kinds of seed-bearing plants, vegetation, and every kind of trees. And he saw that all this, too, "was good."

On the fourth, he put two great lights in the dome of the sky to give light to the earth and separate day from night and to be signs for the days and seasons of the year. The greater light (Sun) would rule by day and the lesser (Moon) by night. He saw that it, too, "was good."

On the fifth, God had the waters bring forth swarms of every kind of living creature, even great sea "monsters," and let winged birds of every kind fly. And so it was. God then blessed them and told them to multiply and fill the waters in the seas and had the birds multiply on the earth. And so it was.

On the sixth day, he had the earth bring forth every kind of land-dwelling living creature, cattle, creeping things, and wild animals. Finally, on the same sixth day, God created humankind in his own image, making them male and female. so that they might be fertile. (Early ancient Israel was an agrarian society and so the notion of fertility was important to their way of living and thinking.)

God also gave humans a godlike, king-like dominion over all he had ordered and had brought forth. He told the first humans they were to have all living things, seed plants, and fruit trees for food. So, God lovingly intended that humankind live in a wonderful habitat, what the second creation story speaks of as a harmonious, heavenly paradise, called Eden.

He also commanded humankind to be fruitful (fertilize), multiply, fill, and subdue all he had made. Again, at the end of the sixth day he declared that all he had done was good, "indeed very good." (Gen 1:31)

On the last (seventh) day, God "rested" but he also again "blessed" and "hallowed" all he had done. There is no indication that there was anything evil, whether physical, psychological, natural, or moral, in what he had brought forth. All that he had ordered had a beautiful orderliness and goodness and enjoyed a wonderful harmony. Nor is there any indication that humans or anything he had brought forth would ever die.

Ethical notions of the first story. They include, as we have noted, the sacredness and goodness of all creation and the special sacredness of humankind, for God had made humans in his own divine image. The story portrays God as a loving God, for he brought forth a habitat that would provide everything humans would need to be happy. He also gave the first humans a godlike, king-like dominion over all he had done. They were to rule over all that the Lord God had made in his stead and use their fertility to be fruitful and multiply, fill the earth, and subdue it. The Hebrew words for "dominion" indicate that humans were to be vice regents and mediators of prosperity. Their mandate was to exercise a king-like reverential care for God's creation, not exploit it.[8] Reverential care fits in well with the ecological concerns many have today.

C. Second Creation Story (Gen 2:4–24)[9]

The second creation story of origins is very different from the first and very andromorphic (human centered). It clearly comes

---

8. It was the well-known biblical scholar, John R. Donahue, S.J. who called the author's attention to this way of understanding human responsibility and accountability. Humans were bearers of the divine image and are to be responsible stewards in the world, until the day that God makes all things anew.

9. Speiser, *Genesis*, 13–15 and Seow, "God, Names of." In the second creation story, and for the most part throughout the Hebrew Scriptures, the name used for God is "Yahweh;" It occurs over 6828 times. This name is translated as "Lord" or "the Lord God." It is also sometimes translated as "Jehovah" (the Latinization of the four consonant of the Hebrew word, JHWH), the name of the Christian sect, Jehovah Witnesses (JeHoWaH). In Greek the word Yahweh

from oral traditions very distinct from those of the first. Like the first, it stresses the "goodness" of creation and the harmonious interrelationships that humans originally enjoyed with all nature, including with other animals.

It opens with the words "These are the generations of the heavens and the earth when they were created" but the text does not explain what is meant by "generations." (Gen 2:4). Again, there is a suggestion of some kind of evolution or step-by-step development of the cosmos. But, whatever the ancient notion of generations might have meant, it certainly was night-and-day different from modern scientific notions of evolution.

Like the first story, the second presupposes a "pre-existing something." It describes this something as a barren, desert-like place where "no plant of the field was yet in the earth and no herb of the field had yet sprung up—for the LORD God had not caused it to rain." However, this barren, desert-like place did have some trees and water welled up from a stream (Gen 2:5–6). Like the first, this story does not indicate how this desert-like place and its trees and stream came to be; they were just there.

However, there was as of yet no human to till the soil. So, unlike the first, the second story begins with the Lord God bringing forth the first human by molding a piece of the earth's clay into the shape of a human and breathing life into it with his own divine breath. And so this human is portrayed as having a very close relationship with the Lord God and seemed to have been destined for immortality.

The Lord God then placed this first human in the paradise garden, called Eden, so that he could till and keep it. He told the first human that he could freely eat of every tree of the garden; but of the tree of the knowledge of good and evil you must not eat, for in the day that you eat of it you shall die" (Gen 2:16b–17).[10]

---

is translated as "*kupios* (Lord) or *theos* (God.).

10. The language the Lord God used in forbidding the man to eat of this

The word, *adam,* though grammatically masculine, also has the generic meaning of "human being."[11] So when first used in the Biblical text, the word had no sexual connotation and is not used as a proper name here or anywhere in the story. Hence, in our analysis, when we first speak of "Adam," the word is used without sexual connotation nor is it used as a proper name

The word *adam* takes on a sexual connotation only after the Lord God brings forth the second human. For then the biblical text has the first human declaring, in rather, poetic language, "This at last is bone of my bones, and flesh of my flesh; she shall be called Woman" (Gen 2:23).

The Hebrew text makes a pun (a wordplay) on the Hebrew words *adam* and *adamah*. The second of these words means arable land/soil. Thus, we have here a fertility image. This imagery stresses the human's relationship to the soil and so again, as in the first creation account, it reflects the agrarian nature of ancient Israelite society.

The story clearly indicates the human's unique, elevated, divine-like status in creation and among other animals and the human's close relationship with divine goodness. The Hebrew text has the Lord God bringing all other animals to the first human so that the human could name them (Gen 2:19–20). As noted before, in the ancient world "naming" was a prerogative reserved for kings.

The second part of the story focuses on the creation of a partner, that is, a companion or helper, for the first human. It has the Lord God saying: "It is not good that the man should be alone; I will make him a helper or partner fit for him" (Gen

---

tree is the same traditional, technical death-penalty language used elsewhere in the Hebrew Scriptures; e.g., see Lev 20:9, 11–12. Coogan, "In the Beginning," 13–14 (esp. note to 2:16–17 in Hebrew Bible section).

11. Our discussion of the word *adam* is based on Anderson, "Adam," 48–50; and Carr, "Genesis," 13–15. The word *adam* is not used as a personal name until Gen 4:1, although many translations of the Bible do translate it as if it were a personal name.

2:18). The partner is not given the named "Eve," which means "life," until the next story (Gen 3:20). Giving him a partner/companion also indicates the Lord God's love and compassion for the first human for God did not want the first human to feel lonely (Gen 2:18).

The Hebrew words used for "partner" (or "companion" and "helper") are *ezer keneghdo*.[12] The word *ezer* appears rarely in the Hebrew Scriptures and when it does it usually refers to God and so connotes authority. However, here (Gen 2:18) the word *ezer* acquires a different connotation by being combined with the Hebrew word *keneghdo*, meaning "like to" or "corresponding to." This Hebrew word combination suggests that the companion the Lord God brought forth shares an equality with the first human, and neither is subordinate to the other.

The Lord God brings forth the partner by putting the first human into a deep sleep and taking a rib from the first human and making it into a woman (Gen 2:21–22). However, it is the first human, not the Lord God, who declares: "This at last is bone of my bone and flesh of my flesh; she shall be called Woman, for she was taken out of Man" (Gen 2:23). Though both were naked, they were not ashamed (Gen 2:25); both clearly had a childlike innocence.[13]

Ethical Notions of the Second Creation Story. Like the first, this story highlights that humans had a divine-like sacredness that elevates them above all else in creation. For the Lord God himself molded the first human out clay and gave life to the molded clay with his own divine breath. He then made

---

12. See Trible, "Eve," 358–59.

13. In his comments on Gen 1:23–25, Carr, *Genesis*, 15, states: "This concluding song praising the woman corresponds to God's concluding affirmation in the first story that God saw all he had created as 'very good' in 1.31. The unashamed nakedness of the man and woman indicates their still innocent, uncivilized status." The next story on the origin of evil explains how humankind came to lose this innocence. (The ancient Israelites tended to see cities as dens of iniquity.)

the human partner/companion by taking a rib out of the first human.

God's special elevation of the first human does not mean that other created things are not also holy, blessed, awe-inspiring, and demanding of reverence. So, the stories are consistent with our talk today of animal rights and the preservation of animal species threatened with extinction or with other ecological concerns that many today have about our created world.

Again, as in the first, the second portrays God as compassionate and loving. Eden was a garden of paradise; it had everything that humans would need and want. As the third story of origins makes clear, there was no need to fear suffering of any kind (physical, emotional, or moral) and humankind was destined for immortality.

Both stories also emphasize the responsibility humans have to care for creation. In the first, God gave humankind dominion over it and told him to make it fruitful and subdue it; in the second the Lord God creates the first human to till and make fertile the soil. Both stress humankind's relationship to all God had created and their duty to care for it. Though neither creation story speaks explicitly of responsibility and accountability nor of immortality, they do speak of a duty to subdue creation and to till the soil. Only in the third story, after the first humans disobey the Lord God's injunction not to eat of the tree of the knowledge of good and evil, is the idea of evil and mortality introduced. We discuss this story in the next section.

D. Third Story of Origins: The Rise of Evil and the Collapse and Disintegration of Harmony (Gen 3:1–24)[14]

This story is not a creation story but a story of the genesis, the becoming, and origin of evil in the cosmos and universe. It is

---

14. The interpretation of this story is based on Carr, *Genesis*, 7–17. and Speiser, *Genesis*, 21–28.

a sophisticated narrative of the collapse and destruction of the harmonious relationships and goodness that had originally marked all that God had brought forth. It narrates the rise of evil, natural, psychological, and moral. However, it never mentions the word "sin."

The imagery of the forbidden tree of the knowledge of good and evil in the midst of the garden of paradise vividly highlights that humans must do everything possible to maintain the goodness, harmony, and orderliness of all the Lord God had made. But they must do it responsibly.

The narrative begins by telling how the "crafty" serpent asked the woman, not yet named "Eve," what the Lord God had told her husband about not eating of one tree in the garden of paradise.[15] Only after eating of the forbidden tree does the first human gain authority over the woman. He does so by naming (a symbol of authority and control) his wife. The word, "Eve," means "life," for as the story tells us, she is the mother of all the living (Gen 3:20).[16]

In responding to the serpent, the woman assumes that the Lord God's injunction to the first human applies also to her. For she replied that the Lord God had told "them" that they could eat of all trees except the one in the middle of the garden, the tree of the knowledge of good and evil. Eve tells the serpent that God said if they ate of or even touched the tree, they would die, and thus lose their immortality (Gen 3:2–3).

The serpent assured the woman she would not die if she ate of it. He said the Lord God had told them that because the Lord God knew that, were they to eat of it, their eyes would be

---

15. Snakes as symbol: in the ancient world snakes were a symbol of wisdom, fertility, and immortality. Only much later did interpreters see the snake as the "devil." Likewise, the Christian idea and doctrine of original sin did not develop until many millennia later and well into the Common Era (CE).

16. The name "Eve" occurs only four times in the Hebrew and Christian Scriptures: Gen 3:20; 4:3, the apocryphal book of Tobit (also spelled as "Tobias") 8:6; and 1 Tim 2:3.

opened and they would become God-like, knowing good and evil. The woman believed the serpent. She also saw that the tree was delightful to look at, good for food, desirable to eat, and eating of it would make her and her husband as wise as God. Thus, her eating of it would be an act of arrogance, an effort to allow her and her mate "to play God" with all that the Lord God had created.

So, she took fruit from the forbidden tree, ate of it, and shared it with her husband who was with her. Immediately the eyes of both were opened and they became aware and ashamed of their nakedness. Thereby they passed from a state of child-like and animal-like innocence to a "civilized" state and capable of experiencing shame. They felt the need to make themselves "civilized" loincloths out of fig tree leaves so that the Lord God would not see their nakedness.

Then they heard the Lord God walking in the garden and both hid in the trees so that the Lord God would not see their nakedness. But the Lord God called out and asked the first human where he was. The man replied that he had hid because he was afraid to be seen naked.

The Lord God asked him who had told him that he was naked? Had he eaten of the forbidden tree? The man replied by blaming the woman, saying that she had given him the fruit and so he ate of it. Next, the Lord God turned to the woman and asked her what she had done. The woman blamed the serpent, saying it tricked her.

Then the Lord God declared the serpent cursed among all the wild animals and it would have to crawl upon its belly and eat the earth's dust all its life. The Lord God also told the serpent that he would put enmity between the serpent and the woman and between all his and the woman's offspring and that the man would strike the serpent's head, and the serpent would strike the man's heel.

The Lord God told the woman that her childbearing would be forever painful and that she would have desire for her husband but he would rule over her. Note that God did not curse the woman but only described what her fate and that of her husband would be.

He told the man that he would have to toil with sweat on his brow until he had returned to the dust of the earth out of which the Lord God had shaped him and that plants of the field would bring forth thorns and thistles. Thus they, and symbolically all humankind, would loose their immortality.

The man's rule over the woman is a tragic indicator of the disintegration of the original harmonious relationship and connectedness between them and all the Lord God had created. It also suggests the divine recognition that there would be a transition to wisdom as humans passed from childhood innocence to adulthood.

The Lord God then drove them from the garden of Eden, thereby stripping them of the immortality they had when living in the paradise of Eden. Unlike all other animals, only humans would be conscious and ashamed of their nakedness.

He told his heavenly court:[17] "See, the man has become like one of us, knowing good and evil" (Gen 3:22). Thus evil, not just moral but also natural, physical, and psychological, entered the cosmos. All the original harmonious relationships among all that the Lord God had brought forth collapsed and disintegrated.

Ethical notions of the third story. Although the man and his wife were expelled from the garden of paradise, the Lord God showed that he was still a compassionate, caring, loving, and forgiving God. For the Lord God replaced their fig loincloths

---

17. The plural "us" probably refers to the divine beings who composed God's heavenly court. A similar reference occurs in the first creation story (Gen 1:26). Perhaps it is also plural because the original story dates back to a period when the Israelites still recognized polytheism.

with full-body garments of skins so that they could better hide their shame-causing nakedness.

The imagery of the forbidden tree of the knowledge of good and evil vividly highlights the seriousness of humankind's duty to exercise their godlike dominion of over all creation in ethically responsible and accountable ways. So, this third story should make us think twice about our arrogant greediness for wealth and for technologies that will make us happy regardless of what it does to our ecology and eventually to human survival.

CHAPTER 4

Jesus, a Person for and with Others
Four Stories from the Gospel of Luke

THIS CHAPTER FOCUSES ON the image of Jesus as a *par excellence* person for others, a compassionate person, a person for and with others. This is how the miracle and parable stories of the New Testament Gospel portray him. Because of its literary quality the Gospel of Luke gives the most vivid picture of Jesus as such a person. This chapter analyzes four stories from Luke's Gospel: one is a miracle story, the other three contain parables. As in the previous chapter, our purpose is not to convert readers to believe in Christian doctrines about Jesus, but only to highlight, in a vividly imaginative way, key elements of the ethical model employed in this book, especially those of compassion, love, and forgiveness. It has five sections, A through E.

A. Introduction: How the Gospels Came to Be

B. A Roman Centurion Sends for Jesus (Luke 7:1–10)

C. Parable of the Good Samaritan (Luke 10:25–37)

D. Parable of the Prodigal Love of a Father for His Two Sons (Luke 15:11–32)

E. A Sinful Woman Loves and Is Forgiven; the Riddle/Parable of Two Debtors (Luke 7:36–50)

A. Introduction: How the Gospels Came to Be

Jesus died about 30 CE. After Jesus' death, many of his followers dispersed throughout the immense Roman empire to spread the "Good News" (that is, to evangelize, from an ancient Greek word meaning to proclaim or spread good news). These followers saw Jesus as the Messiah, the deliverer of the Jewish people promised for centuries by the prophets of old. They wanted to win followers who would be as enthusiastic about Jesus as they were.

Since few people of that age could read, all the preaching was oral; nothing was put in writing. Eventually, however, (as scholars today hypothesize) some people did make a few tiny written collections of the stories the first evangelists told about Jesus. None of these collections has survived. But it is clear that the authors of the Gospels had access to a few of these collections, though not always to the same ones because of the many similarities found in the Gospels. Scholars calculate that the first Gospel, Mark, was not written until between 66 and 70 CE, some thirty to forty years after Jesus' death. The other Gospels were probably not written before 90 to 100 CE.

Like homilists and preachers today, the first "evangelists" told and retold their stories about Jesus as best as they could remember them and did not hesitate to modify them to suit the needs and interests of the audiences they were addressing. The stories included some words of Jesus, but above all they stressed his miracles and parables. The goal was not to write a historical record of Jesus' life or of his exact words and deeds, but to make converts, just as preachers do today. So, the Gospels are not and were not intended to be biographies of Jesus; rather they were exhortations meant to recruit more followers of him.

The Gospels narrate seventy miracle stories; some twenty-five are repeated (each with different details) in more than one Gospel.[1] In addition to miracle stories, the Gospels narrate thirty distinct parable stories, some of which are also repeated in more than one Gospel (again each with somewhat different details).[2]

B. A Roman Centurion Sends for Jesus (Luke 7:1–10)[3]

The centurion story is the first of a series of episodes that highlight the reception Jesus received from various persons and groups during Jesus' Galilean ministry. The keynote of the stories and episodes is found in Luke 7:16–17, which reads: "They glorified God, saying, 'A great prophet has arisen among us!' and 'God has looked favorably on his people!' This word about him spread throughout Judea and all the surrounding country."

The story is about the admiration that an unnamed Roman centurion had for Jesus because of what the centurion had heard about him. When Jesus was on his way to Capernaum, this centurion heard of his coming and wanted Jesus' help for his sick servant.[4] He sent to Jesus some Jewish elders (leaders), who also clearly felt highly of Jesus, to ask Jesus to come to his home and heal the servant.

When the elders arrived, they earnestly appealed to Jesus by telling him that the centurion was "worthy" of Jesus' attention, for this centurion "loves our people" (that is, loves his neighbor). For he had built a synagogue for them.

---

1. For a list of the miracle stories, see Boring, "Matthew's Gospel," 241–51.

2. For a list of the parables, see Throkmortin, *Gospel Parallels*, 212.

3. Fitzmyer, *Gospel according to Luke I–IX*, 647–53; Culpepper, "Gospel of Luke," 154–57.

4. A centurion was either an employee of the Roman governor Herod Antipas, a member of the Roman police force, or an officer in the custom service. He commanded a company of one hundred soldiers. There is a different and shorter version of this story in the Gospel of Matthew, 8:1–4.

But while Jesus was still on his way, the centurion had second thoughts and sent a second message to Jesus, telling Jesus not to trouble himself to come to his (the centurion's) home because he (the centurion) was not worthy enough to have Jesus enter his home and ought not to have asked him to do so.

In his message the centurion explained that he (the centurion) too was a man with authority. He had soldiers under his command and needed only to say the word and they would do his bidding. He knew that Jesus, too, needed only to say the word, even from afar, and his servant would be cured. The gentile Roman centurion clearly had heard enough about Jesus to have great faith in him.

Upon receiving the second message, Jesus expressed to his followers his amazement of the centurion's humility and told the crowd following him that even in Israel he had never seen such great faith. Upon returning, the Jewish elders found that the servant was once again in good health. For Jesus had indeed healed the servant from afar.

The centurion story highlights that both Jesus and the centurion were persons of compassion. It also teaches that there were not only many Jews who stood in admiration of Jesus but that even some gentiles thought very highly of him.[5]

C. Parable of the Good Samaritan (Luke 10:25–37)[6]

The messages of this parable are: love of neighbor, overcoming prejudices and enmities, the importance of compassion and of identifying with the feelings of others, and avoiding legalistic

---

5. We might consider gentiles the ancient counterparts of today's secular people. The apostle Paul, though himself a Jew, considered himself primarily an "apostle to the Gentiles" (Rom 11:13). Apparently, some gentiles too (like many seculars of today) were "religious" persons, even though they never really signed up as followers of Jesus.

6. See Donahue, *Gospel in Parable*, 129–34; Culpepper, "Gospel of Luke," 226–32, and Donahue, "Parables," 575–78.

and rigid interpretations of ethical norms. In brief, we should be persons for and with others and not lay insupportable burdens on them through the ways we think about and apply ethical norms. We need to be understanding and lovingly forgiving. (For a case study in how to apply compassion when interpreting civil law, see chapter 8 where we examine how the US Supreme Court did so in its ruling on same-sex marriage.)

Jesus told the Good Samaritan parable in response to a question from an expert in Jewish law.[7] The expert wanted to call into question Jesus' authenticity. as a Jew and to reveal Jesus as a hypocrite who did not respect Mosaic law. (But in the end, it was the expert who turned out to be the hypocrite.)

The expert asked Jesus, "What must I do to inherit eternal life?" Jesus countered by asking the lawyer, "What is written in the Law?" The lawyer answered: "You shall love the Lord your God with all your heart, and with all your soul, and with all your strength, and with all your mind; and your neighbor as yourself." Jesus told him that his answer was correct. Then Jesus told the Good Samaritan parable.

The story revolves around three figures: a Temple priest, a Levite (an assistant to Temple priests), and a Samaritan. The focus is on the Samaritan and his actions, not on the man he helped.

The Samaritan was traveling along the road from Jerusalem to Jericho. In Jesus' time it was considered a lonely and dangerous road; there were many bandits along it. He came across a man who had been beaten, robbed, stripped of his clothes, and left half dead on the roadside. The man had nothing on him

---

7. There was a long history of hatred between Jews and Samaritans. For example, after the Babylonian exile, the Samaritans opposed the restoration of the Jerusalem Temple; in the second century BCE they helped Syria in wars against the Jews; and in the early first century of the Common Era (CE) they defiled the Jerusalem Temple by scattering human bones in it, thereby preventing the Passover celebration. So, in Jewish eyes, Jesus' negative comparison of the Samaritan traveler with a Jewish priest and Levite was shockingly unacceptable. See Donahue, *Seek Justice*, 196–202.

that might identity who he was, such as his religious identity or whether he could afford medical care and other assistance. Two members of the Jewish religious establishment, a priest and a Levite, had come across the man but, upon seeing him, crossed to the other side of the road to avoid him.

When the Samaritan saw him, he was filled with compassion. So he stopped and bandaged up the badly beaten man. He then brought him to an inn and paid the innkeeper to care for him. He also promised to reimburse the innkeeper for any additional expenses incurred for his care.

After finishing the parable, Jesus asked the lawyer which of the three was a neighbor to the beaten man. Of course the lawyer had no choice but to say, "The one who had mercy on him." Jesus told him, "Go and do likewise" (Luke 10:37).

D. Parable of the Prodigal Love of a Father for His Two Sons (Luke 15:11–32)[8]

The traditional title of this parable is "the Prodigal Son." But the traditional title distorts the message of the parable; for the real focus of the parable is on the father. Observe that the Gospel account begins with the words, "There was a man who had two sons," thereby putting the principal focus on "the man," that is, on the father.

Moreover, the most important message of the parable lies in the attitudes and actions of the father. It is highlighted in his distinct responses to each son. It was one of understanding, love, forgiveness, and compassion. One scholar has suggested the parable's title should stress the father's love. The father's love is "prodigal" because of the extravagant, forgiving

---

8. See Donahue, *Gospel in Parable*, 151–58. I am indebted to Donahue for all the details he provided on this parable; see also to Fitzmyer, *Gospel according to Luke X–XXIV*, 1083–92.

understanding he shows each son. Hence, we entitle it, "the Parable of the Prodigal Love of a Father for His Two Sons."

The parable has three acts: The first (Luke 15:11–19) focuses on the departure and fall of the younger son. That may explain its traditional title, "The Prodigal Son"; the second (Luke 15:20–24) focuses on the son's return and the welcome his father gave him; and the third (Luke 15:25–32) focuses on the reaction of the older son. All highlight the father's responses to each son. Each act begins by naming the main figure of its particular act, the younger son, the father, and the older son.[9]

The reader may find the two sons evoking the most emotional drama: sympathy for the first and anger for the second. But readers should not allow their emotional reactions to the two sons to prevent them from capturing the deepest message of the parable. Again, it is the father's distinct responses to each son that shape the drama both by what he says and by what he does (15:22, 27, 30–31).

Act 1: Departure and Fall of the Younger Son (Luke 15:11–19). In Jesus' time, only about a half million Jews lived in Palestine. Most Jews, about four million, lived in Hellenistic diaspora communities in other parts of the Roman Empire, which extended from Persia to Rome. Because the Palestinian agrarian economy was precarious, many younger Jewish sons migrated to other parts of the empire in hopes of finding a better life. For this reason, the younger son's request for his share of the inherence should not be seen as a rebellion against his father or as a desire for unwarranted freedom. Also, Jewish law permitted a father to dispose of his property during his own lifetime.

Nor was it improper for a son to ask for his share of the father's inherence before the father died. But if a son did receive it, it was understood that what he received was not totally at his disposal. The son was allowed to invest the capital he received

---

9. Donahue, *Gospel in Parable*, 152.

and use it to earn more income. However, he was not to jeopardize its principal; he was expected to keep it within the family circle so that it would be available for assisting his parents, if necessary, in their old age.

The younger son did not do this. Soon after receiving his inheritance, he departed for a far-off country. Instead of looking for better prospects, the younger son decided his fate by squandering his property in dissolute living. After he had spent all his inheritance, a famine arose. In desperation, he chose to work for a gentile by tending to pigs, a ritually unclean animal under Jewish law. He became so hungry that he would have gladly eaten the same food as the pigs, but no one gave him anything.

For a Jewish audience, working for a gentile and feeding religiously unclean pigs were worse than physical death. Jews in the diaspora communities did have systems for giving alms to travelers and émigrés, but the Gospel story suggests that the younger son did not seek their assistance. Yet, even if he had, he perhaps would not have received any help since his situation was his own fault. In any case, he apparently did not seek help from the Jewish community. Instead, he chose to work for a gentle and tend to the religiously unclean. Clearly, the son had soon lost all familial, ethnic, and religious identity.

Finally, the son came to his senses and had a change of heart, but in a somewhat self-serving way. Fearing death, but hoping for something better, he decided to return to his father and confess: "I have sinned against heaven and before you; I am no longer worthy to be called your son; treat me like one of your hired hands" (Luke 15:18–19).

Act 2: The Younger Son's Return and His Father's Welcoming of Him (Luke 15:20–24). While the younger son was still far away, his father spotted him and was filled with compassion. At once, the father ran to him and embraced and kissed him. When they met, the younger son immediately began his prepared confession, but his father cuts him short, for Luke's narrative dramatically leaves out the last words that the son had put in his prepared confession: "treat me like one of your hired hands." (Cf. Luke 15:19, 21.)

In welcoming back his wayward son, the father at once gives a flood of orders to his slaves: they were to clothe the wayward son in his father's best robe, put the family ring on his finger and sandals on his feet, have a fatted calf killed, and prepare a banquet to celebrate the son's return.

The account has the father proclaiming, "This son of mine was dead and [now] is alive again; he was lost and is found" (Luke 15:24). The rapid flurry of the father's actions to welcome back his son contrasts sharply with the younger son's rapid downfall.

The ring the father had put on the younger son's finger symbolized that the younger son could now act in the household with the same authority as the father. Since the narrative omits the last part of the son's prepared confession, it shatters any suggestion that the son would be considered a hired servant, much less a slave. In this sense, the son's intended request to have his father treat him as his hired hand was neither listened to nor granted; rather it was transcended.

The father's rapid actions suggest that the son, at least symbolically, was raised to a higher position than the one he had prior to his departure with his share of the father's property.

Act 3: Reaction of the Older Brother and the Father's Response (Luke 15:25–32). This act also begins with a return—the return of the older brother from the fields. When he returned, he found a big celebration already in full swing, "with music and dancing." He asked a slave what was going on. When he found out, the older son got angry and refused to go in. His father came out and tried to explain and pleaded with him for loving understanding.

But the older son immediately and angrily retorted:

> "Listen! For all these years I have been working like a slave for you [thus comparing himself to a slave, not to a hired hand] and I have never disobeyed your command; yet you have never given me even a young goat so that I might celebrate with my friends. But when this son of yours came back, who has devoured your property with prostitutes, you killed the fatted calf for him!" (Luke 15:29–30)

Observe that the older son referred to himself as the father's son and avoided any reference to the younger son as his brother.

The father remonstrated: "Son, you are always with me and all that is mine is yours. But we had to celebrate and rejoice, because this brother of yours was dead and has come to life; he was lost and has been found" (Luke 15:31). Observe that, in contrast to his elder son, the father refers to the younger son explicitly as the "brother" of the older.

Again, the ring the father had put on the younger son's finger symbolized that the younger son was a full and equal member of the family. The father invited the older son to recognize the younger brother as such and thereby preserve the oneness of family relationships. The father saw both sons as having equal authority and dignity. Thus, the parable has the father countering the anger and divisive language of the older brother with the language of reconciliation and unity. Finally, as previously observed, the father's rapid actions cut off any opportunity for the younger brother to self-identify in any servile way. Rather, in his responses to each son, the father sought to maintain the dignity and unity of the family.

The father's behavior reflects what Jesus, the person for and with others, represents: a person of compassion, understanding, and loving forgivingness, one who seeks to overcome divisiveness and prejudices. This is the image of Jesus that Luke portrays throughout his Gospel.

E. A Sinful Woman Loves and Is Forgiven: the Riddle/Parable of the Two Debtors (Luke 7:36-50)[10]

This story is incredibly complex, yet succinctly and magnificently told. It involves notions of faith, peace, love, and forgiveness. It portrays Jesus as a person for and with others, a person full of love and forgiveness, a person of deep understanding, full of compassion with and for others, always available, and committed to do all one can to help others.

It also pictures Jesus as a person who recognizes that we humans live in a very messy, nitty-gritty world and must avoid judging others by imposing our own ethical norms and mores on them, especially if they are marginalized and live, often unavoidably so, in very different situations as compared with those of mainstream society.

Previous units of this chapter in Luke's Gospel portrayed Jesus as one greater than a prophet by comparing and contrasting him with the Hebrew prophets of old and to John the Baptist and his preaching (Luke 7:11-35). This point is important because the story examined here culminates the chapter and further highlights points made about Jesus in previous units of Luke's Gospel. The story makes clear that Simon, the banquet host, and probably the other guests, too, were well aware that many of Jesus' followers were beginning to see Jesus in this way, that is, not just as another prophet, but a prophet greater than the ones of old. The actions and words of Jesus in the story accord with such a portrayal and further highlight it.

This growing respect for Jesus may have been Simon's motive for inviting Jesus to have dinner with him and his fellow Pharisee's friends. They were curious to know more about him while at the same time at least a little disparaging of him .

We discuss this Lukan story in three stages and conclude our discussion with some spiritual reflections on it.

---

10. Fitzmyer, *Gospel of Luke, I-IX*, 683-692; Culpepper, "Gospel of Luke," v. 9, 167-173; and Soards, "Gospel According to Luke,," 1881-82.

Stage One, the Setting (Luke 7:36–39). Simon is clearly a wealthy Pharisee. His home appears to have a large courtyard that uninvited townspeople can easily intrude. The guests undoubtedly reclined with outstretched feet around a large banquet table.

An unnamed outlandish woman, who at least mainstream Jewish society shunned and considered a sinner, intrudes in the courtyard. The text does not explain in what way she was a sinner nor how she came to know Jesus. (Perhaps she was just someone in the crowds that followed Jesus.) However, clearly her sociocultural situation was difficult. She clearly loved Jesus and came well prepared with a alabaster jar of perfumed ointment, intent on tearfully washing, anointing, and kissing Jesus' feet and drying them with her hair.

The text portrays Simon as thinking to himself that "If this man were a prophet, he would have known who and what kind of woman this is who is touching him—that she was a sinner (Luke 7:39).

We can well understand that when a commonly regarded "sinful" woman entered Simon's house and started doing the things she did, Simon would have been scandalized and felt himself and all his household dishonored, especially given the importance of honor, shame, and family name in the Middle East of that day.

Worse, this commonly regarded and supposedly "sinful" woman did not even ask Jesus permission to do what she did, and, even worse from a Jewish perspective, Jesus made no effort to stop her. She just came in, stood at Jesus' feet, and tearfully started washing and drying them with her hair, and then kissing and anointing them with the ointment she brought with her.

Stage Two, the Riddle Parable (Luke 7:40–43). Jesus clearly intuited Simon's thoughts and askes Simon if he could say something. Simon, addressing Jesus as "teacher," tells Jesus to speak. Jesus then proposes a riddle parable. (Proposing riddles at banquet-like suppers were a common form of dinner entertainment in Jesus' day.)

Jesus then says: "A certain creditor had two debtors; one owed five hundred denarii, and the other fifty. When they could not pay, he canceled the debts for both of them" (Luke 7:41–42). He asked Simon which of them might love him more? Simon, perhaps sensing a trick, cautiously answered, "I suppose the one who had the bigger debt forgiven." Jesus tells him that was correct.

Then Jesus looked at the woman and said to Simon:

> "Do you see this woman? I entered your house; you gave me no water for my feet, but she has bathed my feet with her tears and dried them with her hair. You gave me no kiss, but from the time I came in she has not stopped kissing my feet. You did not anoint my head with oil, but she has anointed my feet with ointment" (Luke 7:44–46).[11]

Stage Three: Jesus' Words about and to the Woman (Luke 7:47–49). Jesus tells Simon that this woman's sins (which are many) are forgiven for she has shown great love. (Note Jesus did not say who had forgiven her sins.) The other guests, misinterpreting what Jesus had said, then began asking one another who was this person who even forgives sins? Jesus then tells the woman, "Your faith has saved you; go in peace" (Luke 7:50).

Spiritual reflections on the story.[12] We fail to hear the message of this story if we fail to find something of ourselves in the character of Simon. This failure happens to the extent that we are blind to our own faults as well as to the horrendous faults of the societal structures of the society and social grouping with which we identify.

---

11. Doing all these things was customary in Jesus' day for a guest invited to dinner.

12. These reflections were inspired by the reflections of R. Alan Culpepper, "Gospel of Luke," 172–73. Culpepper is clearly indebted to Fitzmyer, *Gospel according to Luke I–IX*, 684–88.

Simon saw himself as blameless and the woman as a sinner. He was quick to judge and condemn both Jesus and the woman. He was like the person in the parable about the Pharisee and tax collector (Luke 18:9–14). In that story both were praying in the temple. The Pharisee, in his prayer, thanked God he was not like such people as thieves, rogues, adulterers, and "tax collectors." In his prayer he reminded God that he fasted twice a week and gave a tenth of his income to the temple. But the tax collector, in his prayer, did not dare even look up to heaven; rather, he beat his heart and breast and prayed, "God be merciful to me, a sinner." In concluding this story, Jesus commented: "I tell you, this man [the tax collector] went down to his home justified rather than the other; for all who exalt themselves will be humbled, but all who humble themselves will be exalted" (Luke 18:14).

Simon's real problem was not his conduct but his attitude and lack of self-understanding as well as a lack of understanding of others. Because Simon thought of himself as a pious and righteous Jew of his society, especially in comparison to the woman and her situation, he believed that both he and mainstream Jewish society of his day had done little that needed forgiveness. As a result, he had had little awareness of what it meant to be loved and forgiven by others (including by God). Receiving forgiveness is a grace whether one sees it as coming from God and from somewhere else.

Unlike the woman, or for that matter, unlike anyone who has had any experience of being marginalized and shunted by mainstream society, Simon also had no experience of being newly accepted back into the human community (which is also God's community) as an equal and in good standing. The marginalized who have been an accepted back into society by others know what it means to have received the grace of being loved and forgiven.

Clearly the unnamed woman felt that Jesus compassionately recognized her marginality and her state of being ostracized.

Jesus did not judge her. He loved her. He accepted her as she was. So she had genuinely experienced the grace of love and acceptance. We may likewise assume that she knew that Jesus treated other marginalized persons the same way. This grace, this experience, enabled her to know the meaning of true love in the sense of both receiving and giving love.

The experience of acceptance without judgment, no matter what our sins or defects are or have been, is a powerful force for new life, for new faith, for salvation, and for peace. Such faith, such salvation, such peace, such new life cannot be faked. Such an experience enables one to see a new sunset, whether they identify with some religious group or are simply secularly religious. But to have such an experience requires absolute, transparent humility.

If we can enable the marginalized to find a new acceptance, we, too, will experience a new sunset and all that comes with it.

Does love lead to forgiveness or vice versa? This story teaches that both are essential. Jesus saw the woman's love as a sign that she had been forgiven much. And, conversely, the fact of her forgiveness led to love. The two responses are inevitably intertwined. There is not one without the other.

Our ethical norms and sociocultural mores must not be of the type that presumes that our own set of ethical norms and mores must also be the norms of others whose messy nitty-gritty, perhaps horrendous, situation in life is not the same as ours.

We must be humble, sensitive, and understanding of persons and societal groupings wherever we find ourselves. We must not see our ethical norms as "one-size-fits-all." Ethical norms and societal-cultural mores, if they are to be useful and effective, must reflect the lived reality of our lives. For their purpose is to enable us to get through the real-life situations we are experiencing. Think of women who must prostitute themselves because they can find no other way to make it through life economically.

In this compassionate and respectful light we must look at those faced with. abortion, family planning, contraception, and human reproduction issues.

CHAPTER 5

Compassion and Respect
Abortion Issues, Part One of Two

THIS CHAPTER AND THE next apply our model for doing ethics to questions raised by abortion. We entitle chapter 5 "Abortion Issues: Part One of Two" and chapter 6 "Abortion Issues: Part Two of Two." Chapter 5 has five sections, A through E.

- A. Abortion: A Divisive, Intractable Issue
- B. Ronald Dworkin: Overcoming Divisiveness by Finding a Mediating Middle Ground for Beginning Public Policy Discussion
- C. The Official Roman Catholic Position on Abortion
- D. Abortion and Compassion: Two Real-life Case Studies, Gustafson and Kaveny
- E. Abortion: Legal Observations: Catherine Kaveny, Ronald Dworkin, and George Dennis O'Brien

A. Abortion: A Divisive, Intractable Issue

Pewforum Reports.[1] As of 2019 support for legal abortion remained as high as it has been in the two previous decades of polling.[2] Sixty-one percent of those polled said that abortion should be legal in all or most cases; in contrast, only 38 percent said it should be illegal in all or most cases. When exceptions are made, they were usually for late-term abortions, rape, forced incest, or when the mother's life is at stake. By gender, men and women had similar views on abortion: 61 percent of men and 60 percent of woman said that abortion should be legal in all or most cases.

Seventy-seven percent of white evangelical Protestants thought it should be illegal in all or most cases; by contrast, 83 percent of the religiously unaffiliated said it should be legal in all or most cases. Sixty-four percent of black Protestants and 60 percent of white mainline Protestants thought it should be legal in all or most cases. Even among Roman Catholics a small majority (56 percent) said that it should be legal in all or most cases same.

By level of education, 70 percent of college graduates and 60 percent with some college education said abortion should be legal in all or most cases. A slim majority (58 percent) of those with a high school degree or less said abortion should be legal in all or most cases, while 40 percent said it should be illegal in all or most cases.

The results of the Pew Research Center reports suggest that we be careful of the impression that some religious leaders and politicians of both parties try to give when interviewed for the news. Their discussions are often politically or religiously slanted and contribute little or nothing to rational public discourse

---

1. See Pew Research Center, "Public Opinion on Abortion."
2. This still holds even though many state legislatures have managed to enact laws that severely restrict abortions or at least make access to them very difficult, especially for the poor.

on the legal and ethical questions about abortion that the public should be informed about.

Number of abortions.[3] The Center of Disease Control reported that in 2016 there were 623,478 legally induced abortions. This data represents an average of 11.5 abortions per one thousand women of that age. It also represents a remarkable 24 percent decrease in the annual number of legally induced abortions from 2007 and 2016. (In 2007 there were 825,240.)

Ethical Aspects: Pro-Life vs Pro-Choice.[4] Abortion is a very divisive, intractable, societal-ethical, public policy controversy, at least in the United States. One reason for this is that the discussion of abortion as an ethical issue has not been limited to scholars and medical practitioners. Many religious and other groups, as well as politicians, the courts, and the general public take extremist and very absolutist positions on abortion. In doing so, many employ very invective language, which may well be described as "prophesy with contempt."[5]

One reason for its intractability is the bitterness (often approaching hatred) between pro-life and pro-choice advocates. Those who speak of themselves as "pro-life," seem to see those who disagree with them as "anti-life" and as promoting a "culture of death." They also consider only the rights of the embryo or fetus. They often base their position on the notion that an embryo is a person from the moment of conception.[6] Pro-lifers also seem lacking in the virtue of compassion in the sense that

---

3. https://www.cdc.gov/mmur/volumes/68/ss/6511a1.htm A. Accessed August 16, 2020. There is no way of knowing the number of illegally induced abortions or the number of miscarriages that occur before a woman knows she is pregnant.

4. Johnson, "Ethical Perspectives."

5. The author got the idea of "prophecy with contempt" from Cathleen Kaveny's book, *Prophecy without Contempt*. We discuss Kaveny's ideas on various of her books in later sections.

6. We consider the fatal weakness of the "person-from-moment-of-conception position in chapter 7 in the section on personhood. It is "fatally" weak because embryology, as a science, cannot support the notion of personhood.

they do not consider the impact a pregnancy may have on lives other than that of the embryo or fetus and so give little weight to the sacredness of other lives.

Pro-choice advocates consider only the pregnant woman. Some proclaim that an embryo and fetus are no more persons than an acorn is a tree.[7] They emphasize the rights and freedom of women. They see anti-abortionists as infringing on these rights. The most extreme do not consider abortion even an ethical issue. They stress that a woman has a natural right to decide to have or not have an abortion and need give no reason. Some see abortion as just another medical or surgical procedure. In contrast to the pro-life advocates, they give little or no weight to the intrinsic (in itself) sacredness of *all* human life, including embryos and fetuses. (We discuss the notion of sacredness in the next chapter.)

Another reason for the intractability is that their positions are often rooted in deeply held moral, religious, or religious-like convictions. It is impossible to rationally argue for or against such convictions. The battle lines drawn by both groups are deeply ideological; they leave little room for rational discussion.

In United States, abortion is one of the most acrimonious public policy issues. All sides in the controversy are so fixated in their positions that rational argument in the public forum is impossible. No side in the controversy seems interested in finding a mediating "middle ground" that would give them a common starting point for rational dialogue about abortion in a public form. We reject such pessimism.

---

7. Dworkin, *Life's Dominion*, 30–31.

B. Dworkin: Overcoming Divisiveness by Finding a Mediating Middle Ground for Beginning Policy Discussion[8]

Dworkin (whom we discuss at much greater length in the next chapter) rejects such pessimism. In his book, *Life's Dominion: An Argument About Abortion, Euthanasia, and Individual Freedom*, he argues that it is possible to find a mediating middle ground from which the various parties in the abortion debate might respectfully start to discuss their differences in the public square. Hopefully, such dialogue will lead to public policy accommodations and compromises. Compromises never fully satisfy anyone but they can allow people to live together with respect for one another and collaborate in many ways to create a more compassionate, peaceful, and better world.

Dworkin argues that the abortion controversy usually centers around the legal and ethical rights of the embryo and fetus versus those of the woman. The notion of rights is a very contentious one, whether from legal, ethical, and philosophical perspectives. Dworkin believes that such a starting point is a "no-go, no-win" one.

To avoid this "no-go, no-win" one, Dworkin proposes as a middle ground in public-policy dialogue the notion of the unique sacredness of all human life. He believes that essentially everyone agrees that all human life has a unique sacredness, even though people have different understandings of the meaning and degrees of life's unique sacredness and their implications.[9] He argues that ultimately both the pro-life and pro-choice positions are rooted in the sacredness of human life. But one focuses exclusively on the sacredness of the life of the embryo and fetus; the other on the sacredness of the life of the pregnant woman.

---

8. Dworkin, *Life's Dominion*, esp. 11–25
9. Dworkin, *Life's Dominion*, 71–84.

Compassion and Respect

Ronald Dworkin sees both the pro-life and the pro-choice positions as simplistic. For him the ethics of abortion is far more complex than either wants to recognize. For him, all forms of human life (including the embryo, fetus, mother as well as others who may be affected if a pregnancy is brought to terms) are uniquely sacred in themselves, although there are degrees to this sacredness. For this reason, in response to both positions, Dworkin holds that every abortion is tragic, bad, and ethically problematic but may be justifiable (perhaps even obligatory) in some situations. In this sense, it is difficult to label Dworkin as either pro-life or pro-choice.

He also argues that both groups ultimately base their position, at least implicitly, on the notion of the unique sacredness of all human life, though they differ in their understanding of this sacredness and its implications. (We address these points in chapter 6.)

To discuss these differences respectfully, participants must at least be open to listening to one another and to trying to understand where the various sides are coming from. They also need to have a sincere desire to respect one another's obligation to follow one's own moral conscience and to be committed, despite their differences, to making efforts to find pragmatic, respectful compromises for living together and collaborating in making for a better world.

People in every society differ on many things but they learn to accommodate one another. Nations regularly draw up peace, trade, and other agreements to end or avoid armed conflict or trade wars. This always requires many tradeoffs; for no side ever gets all it would like.[10]

To be concrete about the *sine qua non* importance of what is meant by respecting the freedom of conscience of others, we discuss in the next section the ways the highly authoritarian

---

10. We have already referred to the tradeoffs the Founding Fathers made in order to get the US Constitution agreed upon.

Roman Catholic Church has, over the centuries, developed for protecting this freedom, at least theoretically.[11] We say "theoretically" because it seems that, in practice, many bishops and priests, as well as many conservative Protestant ministers, sweep the notion of freedom of conscience under the carpet for fear that, if people in the pews come to know of its implications, many might fall onto the slippery path to perdition.

C. The Official Roman Catholic Position on Abortion[12]

Our purpose in discussing the official Catholic position at some length is not to challenge it or advocate it but because it is the clearest, most nuanced statement of the pro-life, anti-abortionist position. (In chapter 6 we will contrast the official Catholic position with Ronald Dworkin's more liberal, less absolutist model.) The nuances of the official Catholic position raise the question of whether its official position is as absolutist as many think it is.

The official Catholic position raises this question because, probably surprisingly to many, it ethically allows two surgical procedures when certain medical conditions endanger the mother's life. It speaks of these allowances as indirect abortions in contrast to direct abortions that intentionally and directly kill an embryo or fetus.

---

11. We examine in detail an example of the nuanced liberal position presented by Ronald Dworkin in the next chapter.

12. For an excellent, in depth, objective précis of the official Catholic position, including its historical development and current teachings, see Cahill "Catholic Perspective," 37–41. Not every Catholic, even the most loyal and practicing ones, fully accept the official Catholic position. We will see this when we examine some positions taken by Roman Catholic philosopher and academic.

Cahill is the J. Donald Monan Professor of Theology at the Roman Catholic Boston College and former president of the Society of Christian Ethics and the Catholic Theological Society of America.

In developing this section, the author had the assistance of several Roman Catholic ethicists who wish to remain anonymous.

COMPASSION AND RESPECT

The procedures are "indirect" because neither procedure intentionally or directly kills the embryo or fetus. However, they do, and unavoidably so, put the embryo or fetus in an environment outside of the mother's body, where it quickly dies. However, the only direct action and intention in these procedures is saving the mother's life, not killing the embryo or fetus. The two procedures are:

First Procedure. If an embryo becomes lodged in the mother's fallopian tube and cannot descend into her womb, it is likely to cause a life-threatening hemorrhage as it grows larger. In this case, the official Catholic position allows a surgeon to remove the section of the fallopian tube above and below where the embryo is lodged as long as (1) neither the mother nor the surgeon "intends" the death of the embryo and (2) the surgery is not performed in a way that directly kills (cuts into) the embryo itself.[13]

Second Procedure. If the womb of a pregnant woman is found to be cancerous, the official Catholic position allows a surgeon to removed her womb as long as the embryo or fetus is not directly or intentionally killed. However, the procedure will unavoidably place the fetus outside of the mother's body where, for lack of nourishment through the umbilical cord, the fetus will die almost immediately.

The philosophical principle that Roman Catholic moralists use to justify these two procedures is called the "double-effect" principle. One effect is evil (death of the embryo or fetus), the other good (saving the mother's life). In both cases, the application of this principle allows the death of an embryo or fetus because the mother's life is threatened. Some criticize this double-effect principle as legal quibbling and "pharisaical."

---

13. Today, rather than surgery, physicians usually address the problem of an embryo lodged in a fallopian tube by administrating a medicine that kills the lodged embryo. However, the Catholic position would not permit the administration of such a medicine since it would directly and intentionally kill the lodged embryo.

Others argue that it would be better to justify the procedures by appealing to the Jesus-like virtues of compassion and understanding. (We discussed these virtues in chapter 4 and elsewhere where we spoke of Jesus as "a person for others.")

The double-effect principle is a moderating influence on the otherwise very absolutist, anti-abortionist Catholic stance. The Catholic theologican Lisa Solle Cahill explains that the premise behind the use of the double-effect principle is that "the woman's life is at least equal in value to that of her unborn offspring."[14] For this reason, a woman has no obligation to risk her life to protect the life of an unborn child. Moreover, neither procedure directly kills the embryo or fetus since there is no intention that the embryo or fetus die and no direct action is taken to kill it. The premise behind the double-effect principle suggests that there are degrees of the unique sacredness of all human life; for in both procedures the mother seems to consider her life as having more importance than that of the embryo and fetus. (We discuss the question of degrees of importance in the next chapter.)

Cahill also cites the 1987 "Instruction" to *Donum Vitae* (*Gift of Life*) of the Vatican Congregation of the Doctrine of the Faith. This document concedes that there is no scientific (embryonic or other) proof that an embryo is a person from the moment of conceptions; however, the Vatican document does plead that the embryo and fetus be given the benefit of the doubt. Critics of this position see this "stance" as no more than an exhortation, not a rational, philosophical argument.[15]

Freedom of Conscience in the Catholic Tradition. In closing this discussion of the official Catholic position, we should also examine the Catholic Church's teachings on the importance of respecting freedom of conscience and the moral duty to always obey one's conscience. Like the double-effect principle, these

---

14. Cahill, "Catholic Perspective," 39.
15. Cahill, "Catholic Perspective," 39

Catholic teachings also provide a moderating influence on its abortion position.

This tradition is well expressed in the *Second Vatican Council's "Declaration on Religious Freedom.*[16] This Declaration very strongly states that no one may ever try to force their moral views on another, whether that other be an individual, a large societal grouping, or something in-between. It reads in part: "in matters religious no one is to be forced to act in a manner contrary to his own beliefs . . . . whether privately or publicly, whether alone or in association with others, within due limits." (An example of a "due limit" might be the case of one who believed it was morally permissible to kill someone trespassing on her/his property.)

For some Catholic ethicists, this document raises the question of what public position the Catholic Church should take in making its anti-abortion teaching the law of the land. To seek to make the Catholic position the law of the land would seem to be an effort to force the Catholic position on others. It would also be contrary to the notion of separation of church and state. Of course, it is not just some Catholics who seem to want to make anti-abortion laws the law of the land; many very conservative Evangelicals also take this position.

Another moderating principle in the Catholic tradition is the principle of *epikeia* (also spelled *epieíkeia*). *Epikeia* is an ancient Greek word meaning reasonableness or fairness. It goes back to Aristotle's *Nicomachean Ethics*. For centuries Roman Catholic Canon lawyers have considered this principle (also spoken of as a virtue) as fundamental to the correct, compassionate interpretation Roman Catholic Canon Law and for respecting the human freedom, dignity, and conscience of others.[17]

---

16. Paul VI, "Declaration of Religious Freedom," 678–679, para. 2.

17. See Coriden et al., *Code of Canon Law*, 1152. This refers to the Code of 1983 that was revised in accord with the Second Vatican Council and promulgated by Pope John Paul II; It went into effect on November 27, 1983. Ladislas

As a virtue, *epikeia* enables Catholic Canon lawyers to avoid the kind of criticisms Jesus levelled against many Pharisees and teachers of Mosaic Law of his day. It holds that no "lawgiver" can foresee every possible aspect of situations where a specific law may seem to apply. Therefore, in applying the law, a canon lawyer must use the virtues of prudence, reasonableness, and compassion when applying the law.

Finally, there is the Roman Catholic moral theology tradition. For example: in response to a question, the most distinguished Roman Catholic theologian of the second half of the twentieth century, Karl Rahner (1904–84), explained this tradition clearly. He said he personally held to the traditional Roman Catholic view on abortion; however, after stating this, Rahner emphatically added that even according to normal Catholic teaching on moral obligation one must always follow one's conscience.[18] And he added that he could conceive of many cases where a person may engage in an abortion in good faith."

He gave this example: If a doctor would have pangs of conscience and feel that he or she would be sinning by not ending a pregnancy prematurely in order to save a mother's life or to prevent some lasting negative impacts on her health, then, in that case, the Catholic moral tradition acknowledges that all persons involved in the abortion acted in good faith (that is, in accord with their consciences) and so would remain in official good standing in the Catholic Church. The same, Rahner added, can be said, of many other moral questions.

Orsy (b. 1921), author of the "Canons and Commentary" chapter in the edited volume cited here, is a renowned expert in Roman Catholic Canon Law. He has been a professor of law at the Law Center of Georgetown University for over 25 years. Though Hungarian by birth, he has long taught in the United States. Recently he and this author had dinner together and he confirmed my understanding of *epikeia*.

18. Rahner, *Faith in a Wintry Season*, 98.

D. Abortion and Compassion: Two Real-life Case Studies, Gustafson and Kaveny

In this section we examine two real-life abortion cases. Hopefully, our consideration of these real-life cases will help keep both our and the reader's feet on the ground and enable a more compassionate understanding of the moral dilemma faced by many women.

The first case was presented by the Protestant moral theologian, James M. Gustafson (b. 1925); the second by the contemporary Catholic theologian/lawyer, Cathleen Kaveny. Among the major points they make is the need for understanding and compassion for the right as well as the duty of a pregnant woman to follow her conscience and to freely make her own decision without pressure from anyone.

Both stress that a pregnant woman must weigh *all* lives that may be affected by carrying a pregnancy to term. This requires a clear, detailed examination of all factors in their cases. Both also clearly think that an abortion might sometimes be justifiable, though this is not to suggest they would agree fully with Dworkin's position. We also remind our readers once again of four points that underlie the argument of our book: (1) we humans are finite and, as discussed in chapter 2, our knowledge of good and evil is very limited and space/time/place bound; (2) to boot, we live in a very messy, nitty-gritty world where our moral choices are often not between a good and an evil, but from among many evils; (3) sometimes we must destroy a life to save other lives, for example, in warfare or in the case of a pregnant woman with a cancerous womb; and (4) finally, an abortion decision must be informed by the virtue of compassion and respect for *all* who may be impacted if a pregnancy is or is not carried to term.

Compassion and Respect

James M. Gustafson, A Woman Pregnant Because of Rape.[19] Gustafson presented this real-life case study as an example of how his own method of doing moral theology differed from the traditional Catholic method of doing moral theology. In doing so, he was not dismissing the Catholic method; for he had close, personal relationships with the greatest Catholic moral theologians of his day and valued greatly their contributions to Christian moral theology.

The woman is in her early twenties. She is unusually intelligent, has an active mind, reads widely, and is quite articulate. Despite her life and present situation, she is not hysterical. She has no physiological problems except for periodic gastrointestinal illnesses, but they would not jeopardize her having a child. She has only two or three friends.

Her mother was an alcoholic who mistreated her and who was given to periods of violence. Her father was a drug addict; he had avoided prison and had managed not to lose his business and so was able to provide a decent income for his family.

However, the woman felt her home had been like a prison. So she fled home after high school to live in a distant state. She no longer has significant contact with her parents or siblings. Clearly, when growing up, she had a tragic and disrupted life.

She had married but after having three children she was divorced by her husband because she had had an affair (now ended) with another man who had "befriended" her, though they never contemplated marriage. Because of her infidelity, her former husband was given legal custody of their three children. She loves and misses her children and carries a heavy guilt load because of her adultery and the lost of her children. She made no excuses for her own adultery.

---

19. Gustafson, "Protestant Ethical Approach," 107–22. Gustafson is a highly renowned, influential, and ecumenical Protestant moral theologian of the second half of the twentieth century to the present. He published eight books on Christian ethics. He has held guest professorial chairs at many universities.

She is now pregnant because she was sadistically and vengefully gangraped by her former husband and three other men. She has no steady job or other source of income. She is unwilling to prefer charges against her former husband for fear it might be detrimental to her children.

She is a lapsed Catholic but had lost confidence in the Catholic Church and its priests, whom she sees as harsh taskmasters. So she is unwilling to turn to them for the spiritual and moral support she now seeks. She no longer has any significant religious affiliation but does feel a need for some "religious" connection. Somehow, she was led to seek spiritual counsel and support from the Protestant moral theologian, James M. Gustafson. Though he is primarily a academic, he is also a Protestant minister and very pastorally oriented.

She has a profound desire to achieve equanimity and end the suffering and conflict in her life. She clearly is not defeated by her past. She has very positive goals she wants to achieve: an aspiration to go to college, become a teacher, or engage in some other kind of professional work, both for her own self-fulfillment and because she wants to make a contribution to others.

She sees abortion as one live option for getting her life together and coping with the pregnancy she now has as a result of violent rapes. But she is also entertaining another option: bringing to term the child she now bears. In speaking to Gustafson, she articulates well this possibility. Especially since she now has been deprived of her first children, she envisions a hope that perhaps she could enable the child she now carries to achieve some realization of her/his goals in life.

So, she has confidence and hopes. She is clearly able to love though she does wonder what more could happen to make her life any more difficult than it has been and is. She does not try to blame others for her situation.

She sees her marriage in early youth as having been part of an effort to free herself from her prison-like parental home. She responds to her rapes more in horror than in hatred but feels herself too close to the horror of that experience to know what their long-term impact may have on her life.

The woman is a clear example of what it means to live in a dirty, messy, nitty-gritty world where the choices available are rarely black and white.

She apparently never asked Gustafson what she should do, but only for moral and spiritual support. She clearly recognizes that she herself must take responsibility and hold herself accountable for whatever she decides. Gustafson also recognizes that in the end only the woman herself has the right to weigh the values and disvalues and alternative options she has and to decide how to responsibly deal with them.

Gustafson sums up his own personal view of her case by saying that he thinks the woman could consider an abortion ethically justifiable for herself. (Of course, in accord with the way he sees his role, he does not share his personal opinion with the woman.) He also adds in a footnote near the end of his article that his method of analysis may also be applicable to cases other than abortion due to rape and "might" lead to similar conclusions in cases of unwed girls and older married women with large families, etc.[20]

As a spiritual counselor, Gustafson sees his role as that of being a good listener and assisting and encouraging her to think though the nitty-gritty dilemmas that challenge her by helping her to clarify her values, convictions, and moral integrity, put them within the framework of a wider moral community of which she is a part, and be aware of all the possible courses of action, the values and disvalues they involve, and the potential consequences of each.

---

20. Gustafson, "Protestant Ethical Approach," 107n4.

COMPASSION AND RESPECT

For Gustafson an ethical counselor's role is not one of judging or prescribing. He also recognizes that, though moral principles are important and at times essential guidelines for moral decision-making, they are not necessarily decisive. Life is too complex and messy for "one-size-fits-all" moral absolutes.

Gustafson writes from the perspective of a Christian ethicist and moralist but much of what he says is applicable to counselors of all faiths and non-faiths, including religious ministers, spiritual directors, physicians, psychologists, nurses, and even friends whose counsel someone may seek. Some professionals may not have the skills that Gustafson has for helping someone seeking their counsel. In such cases, they ought to be able to make referrals to someone who does have such skills.

At the end of his account, Gustafson explains how he arrives at his conclusion as follows: (1) clearly logic alone is not the way to address the woman's predicament; (2) nor are facts alone sufficient to justify an abortion; (3) nor is it a matter of being inspired by the Holy Spirit; it is a human decision made in freedom and informed and governed by beliefs and values.[21]

Concluding Comments by the Author of this Book. Gustafson's pastoral method is similar to the well-known and highly respected nondirective, client-centered therapy approach developed by the US psychologist Carl R. Rogers (1902–87).[22] Rogers's method emphasizes that a counselor must develop a person-to-person relationship between her/himself and the client and encourage the client to search for her/his own solutions to the problems she/he must deal with. The counselor's job is not to solve the client's problem; rather to help the client to think through her/his problem and solve it for her/himself.

---

21. Gustafson, "Protestant Ethical Approach," 117.

22. See Rogers, *Client-Centered Therapy*. This book is a collection of eleven articles that explain how client-center therapy is understood today, what its implications are for psychological theory, and how it is being made use of in play therapy, group-centered psychotherapy, leadership and administration, student-centered teaching, and training of counselors and therapists.

Gustafson also emphasizes that when someone shares personal information and seeks counsel from another, the counselor and client initiate an interpersonal, inter-subjective relationship.[23] So it is important that both counselor and client be open to, and have a measure of confidence in, one another. At the same time, the counselor must maintain a certain professional objectivity to be truly helpful.

The counselor should develop a real empathy, a feeling with and for the client. Additionally, s/he may come to have some responsibility to make her/himself available should the client need future follow-up help. If need be, the counselor ought to be able to refer the client to others with different skills.

Gustafson recognizes that, though moral principles are important and at times essential guidelines for moral decision-making, they are not necessarily decisive. Life is too complex and messy for "one-size-fits-all" moral absolutes. In the end humans must decide how to apply them to each concrete, given situation.

What Gustafson writes is consistent with the notion of contextual (relative/relational) truth that we developed in chapter 2 of this book.

Cathleen Kaveny: A Postpartum Psychotic Woman, Mine Ener.[24] Kaveny briefly reports on the case of the late Mine Ener

23. Gustafson, "Protestant Ethical Approach," 108–9.

24. Kaveny, *Culture of Engagement*, 146–48. Since 2014 Kaveny has been the Darald and Juliet Libby Professor of Theology and Law at Boston College, Chestnut Hill, MA, with joint appointments in both the department of theology and the law school. To date, Kaveny has published four books, all of which we cite in various parts of this book. She has also published over a hundred articles and essays in journals and books specializing in law, ethics, and medical ethics.

After law school she clerked for John T. Noonan Jr., a judge on the US Ninth Circuit Court of Appeals. Afterward, she worked as an associate at the Boston law firm of Ropes & Gray in its health law group. She is chair of the board of trustees of the *Journal of Religious Ethics*. She has been president of the Society of Christian Ethics, which meets annually in conjunction with the Society of Jewish Ethics and the Society for the Study of Muslim Ethics.

who had been Professor of Arab and Islamic Studies at the Roman Catholic Villanova University (Pennsylvania). A year after her marriage, she gave birth to a daughter, Raya Donagi. The child was born with severe down syndrome and related complications. In spite of her child's condition, Mine was determined to give her baby the best possible life. However, she did not have the emotional wherewithal (strength to do so).

Of course, the child's condition did not improve and her mother, Mine, sank ever more deeply into a postpartum depression. By the time Raya was nine months, her mother's depression had become a deep psychosis and she killed her child because, as she told police, she could no longer bear letting the baby continue to suffer. A few weeks later Mine killed herself.

The Villanova community was shocked and heartbroken but did not wish to reduce the meaning of her life to the despair, psychosis, and violence that plagued her last days. So, it erected a plaque in her memory. It was to remind the Villanova community of the overall meaning of her life; the plaque represented a community's act of hope and a prayer for peace.

In examining her case, Kaveny asks, "What was going on?" Catholic teaching condemns murder and suicide. But its teaching also recognizes that it was unlikely that Mine could be judged morally culpable for what she had done. Mine's lengthy and never-improving ever deepening postpartum psychosis had deprived her of the minimum conditions of reason and free will.

Kaveny sees Mine's story as a perfect advertisement for Planned Parenthood: a successful thirty-seven-year-old professional woman who apparently did not receive medical advice to have an amniocentesis.[25] If Mine had had the procedure, she

---

25. Amniocentesis is a procedure that surgically inserts a hollow needle through the abdominal wall and into the uterus to obtain a sample of the amniotic fluid surrounding and protecting the fetus. This fluid contains fetal cells and various proteins and, among other conditions, can detect chromosomal abnormalities such Down syndrome. See Mayo Clinic, "Amniocentesis."

probably would have learned of the fetus's condition. Then she could have elected to have an abortion and perhaps someday give birth to another, but this time healthy, baby.[26]

Kaveny next asks: How might pro-lifers respond to this tale? She suggests three possible responses: first, some might denounce her as a moral monster and see her morally responsible for the tragedy; second, others might recognize that she was a victim trapped by her hormones and destabilized psyche and so would not condemn her to hell. However, such persons would not have "honored" her with a plaque (as the Villanova faculty had done), but rather might see Mine as a freakish "outlier," an anomaly, and would like her to disappear so that they would not have to think much about her "plight." The trouble with this approach, Kaveny says, is that it falsifies reality. Humans don't like to think about life that way. We prefer to think that life will ultimately and always work out for the best if we keep at it, but that is often an illusion, a nonreality; for often things don't turn out that way.

Third, the one Kaveny sees as the most realistic is to recognize that life is morally very messy and much in life is a mystery but accompanied by the hope that there will be in the end a redemption, not just from sin, but also from sorrow and death. This is Kaveny's approach; it is quite faith-driven and theologically based.

Compassion. These case studies illustrate compassion in action. Like the Jesus we discussed in the previous chapter, both Gustafson and Kaveny demonstrate a feeling with and for the

---

26. Kaveny's position on abortion is very complex. In her book, *Law's Virtues*, published two years after *A Culture of Engagement*, she devotes a whole chapter ("The Pro-life Movement and the Purpose of Law," 71–96) to the abortion issue. Her position seems to be not as "liberal as those of Gustafson or Dworkin. She concludes the chapter by saying: "While the right to life may be 'fundamental' in the order of logic, the order of practicality demands a multifaceted strategy to protect that right in Western liberal democracies where abortion has long been legal and widely used . . . Too narrow a strategy will backfire and end up harming rather than promoting the overall well-being."

persons each discusses. They are nonjudgmental, loving, and forgiving.

E. Abortion: Legal Observations: Catherine Kaveny, Ronald Dworkin, and George Dennis O'Brien[27]

Given the divisive views held by people on abortion and given the need to respect everyone's freedom of conscience and their obligation to follow that conscience, these three intellectuals hold that it would be ethically irresponsible, both for us as individuals and for us as a society, to advocate passing legislation or to seek judicial rulings that abolish essentially all abortions. The most notable exception might be late-term abortions that do not pose a danger to the life or well-being of the mother.

In her book, *Law's Virtues*, Kaveny argues that the function of good law is to promote virtue in society. In making legislation and legal rulings in cases of abortion, lawmakers and judges should use the principles of prudence, justice, solidarity, and autonomy and take into consideration the political and societal context of their times and places.[28]

Religious leaders and ordinary citizens should also promote these virtues. If they fail to do so, they may advocate laws and the legal rulings that are likely to promote societal divisiveness, and even lawlessness, rather than societal harmony, justice, and respect for the dignity and freedom that all people have a right to.

Kaveny concludes one chapter of her book ("The Pro-life Movement and the Purpose of Law") by saying that the right to life may be logically fundamental, "practicality demands a multifaceted strategy, especially in Western liberal democracies where abortion has long been legal and widely used. One that

---

27. It is beyond the scope of this book to go in detail into the legal aspects of abortion.

28. Kaveny, *Law's Virtues*, 71–96, esp. 88–91.

is too narrow may "backfire and end up harming rather than promoting the overall well-being."[29]

Kaveny also argues that laws passed to end essentially all abortions do not and cannot really achieve their objectives. Instead, they lead to the establishment of many unregulated, ill-equipped underground clinics with inadequately qualified staff. It is to such clinics that the poor and teenage girls are forced to go. More economically comfortable pregnant women evade such antiabortion laws by going to a state whose laws regulate abortion in more compassionate and medically safe ways.

In other words, any effort to ban or criminalize abortion would be difficult to enforce, especially first-trimester ones. She suggests we think about the mistaken effort to ban the use of alcohol in the early twentieth century.

Even Pope John Paul II, Kaveny observes, recognized the difficulty of doing so in secular, pluralistic societies.[30] He said that religious and political leaders should be realistic about what is attainable. Kaveny comments that it is often not realistic to urge women facing a pregnancy crisis to just put their newborn babies up for adoption. Societies should also accept that substantial assistance programs are both a moral and practical imperative. She closes her discussion by emphasizing that justice should be understood as solidarity, meaning that "our legal systems cannot rightly allow family members to bear the entire burden of caring for the most vulnerable members of society," especially newborns with congenital problems.[31] (We return briefly to this last point again in our closing chapter 8.)

The late constitutional jurist and philosopher, Ronald Dworkin, also opposed the criminalization of abortion. He devotes three chapters to the study of the legal issues raised

---

29. Kaveny, *Law's Virtues*, 91.

30. Kaveny, *Law's Virtues*, 89–91. Her reference to Pope John Paul II is to his 1995 encyclical *Evangelium Vitae* (*Gospel of Life*), para. 72. See her endnote 28 (Kaveny, *Law's Virtues*, 94).

31. Kaveny, *Law's Virtues*, 90–91.

by abortion. He bases them largely in the principle of religious freedom found in the first amendment of the US Constitution. It is beyond the scope of this book to discuss his legal arguments; our interest is in his philosophical positions.

Like Kaveny, the Roman Catholic intellectual and educator, George Dennis O'Brien, in his book, *The Church and Abortion: A Catholic Dissent*, also strongly opposes laws that criminalize abortion because highly restrictive anti-abortion laws cannot work.[32] There is just too much divisiveness in our society on this question. Such laws just lead those who can afford it to go to another state; those who can't afford it, such a teenage girls, go to often ill-equipped, unsafe, illegal underground clinics.

Though he holds with Gustafson, Kaveny, and Dworkin that abortion is intrinsically evil, O'Brien, like them, believes it is sometimes "ethically excusable" and stresses the importance of compassion.[33]

A very persuasive article that argues against the criminalization of abortion is Caitlin Flanagan's "The Things We Can't Face."[34] She see abortion as tragic, even more so than Dworkin, but she vividly highlights the likely dire consequences of making it illegal. Also, like Dworkin, she stresses the sacred humanity of an embryo from the moment of conception (but without calling it a "person") and how quickly the fetus takes on a human form as can be seen in the vivid images that modern technology often painfully makes clear.

---

32. O'Brien, *Catholic Dissent*, 24–26, 120, and. O'Brien has a PhD in philosophy from the University of Chicago) and was successively president of Bucknell University and the University of Rochester, each for about then years.

33. See especially O'Brien, *Catholic Dissent*, ix–x and 83–90.

34. Flanagan, "Things We Can't Face," 72–77.

CHAPTER 6

Compassion and Respect
Abortion Issues, Part Two of Two

CHAPTER 6 CONTINUES OUR discussion of abortion. For this reason, we entitle it chapter 6, "Abortion Issues, Part Two of Two." It has four sections, A through D.

A. Introduction: Morality of Abortion, Dworkin's Goal

B. Dworkin: The Unique Sacredness of All Human Life

C. Dworkin on the Morality of Abortion; For Clarity of Exposition We Present Dworkin's Position in Three Units

D. Real-life Examples of How Handicapped Children Have Coped.

A. Introduction: Morality of Abortion, Dworkin's Goal[1]

To repeat what we have stated before, Dworkin's goal, as well as ours, is to find an acceptable middle-ground that gives all sides in the abortion controversy a common starting point for respectful dialogue in a public forum about their differences. Hopefully, such dialogue will lead to some mediating public policy compromises and accommodations.

---

1. Dworkin, *Life's Dominion*, 30–67.

COMPASSION AND RESPECT

Readers should recall what we said in chapter 1. The Founding Fathers of our nation successfully worked out many compromises that enabled all thirteen original colonies to ratify the US Constitution within a short period. The compromises were both political and ethical. Politically, they created two branches of the federal legislature. They reached a compromise on the very divisive issue of slavery. Within two years, they also passed the first Constitutional amendment which guarantees all citizens and noncitizens freedom of speech and the right to practice or not practice any religion they choose. For freedom of speech and these reasons, Dworkin believes it is not too much to ask that similar compromises be reached on abortion.

Section "B" of the chapter explains what Dworkin means by "sacredness" in general and the "unique" sacredness of all forms of human life (from embryo to birth and until death He argues that the notion of the unique sacredness can serve as a mediating middle-ground starting point for public dialogue on abortion.

Section "C" of the chapter presents Dworkin's discussion of the morality of abortion; it is incredibly complex and often not expressed with sufficient clarity and conciseness. His presentation is clearly meant for philosophers and Constitutional lawyers.[2] Here we try to present his argument in a way that, without oversimplifying it, does not require readers to have had any previous study in philosophy, law, or ethics. We also deal only with its ethical aspects, not its legal ones. For clarity of presentation we divide section "C" into three units.

Dworkin's position represents a contrasting view to the official Catholic position. It is not our purpose to defend or reject either position. Both positions are very nuanced in comparison

---

2. Dworkin devotes five chapters to abortion in *Life's Dominion*; three deal with the Constitutional legal issues; the other two with the philosophical/ethical issues. We consider only the ethical issues and so focus on chapters 2 and 3 (Dworkin, *Life's Dominion*, 30–101).

to the ways most pro-life and pro-choice advocates present their positions.

B. The Unique Sacredness of All Human Life[3]

Dworkin uses the words "intrinsic value," "holiness," "sanctity," "inviolability," and "sacredness" interchangeably. This section explains what Dworkin means by the intrinsic sacredness of life. The notion that some things have intrinsic value in themselves and so are sacred is commonplace among humans. For example, we speak of the sacredness of works of art, beautiful mountain views, animal species, and certain trees and plants and regret if they are seriously damaged or, in the case of animal species, if they become extinct.

Essentially everyone agrees that human life has a unique there are both religious and secular reasons for these conviction. However, there are disagreements about how to understand this sacredness and its degrees of sacredness. (We discuss what Dworkin means by "degrees" of human life's unique sacredness in unit 2 of the next section.) There are both religious and secular reasons for our convictions about the unique sanctity of all human life in all its forms, including the human embryo.

Margaret A. Farley stresses that every form of sexual activity should be seen as sacred. Couples who engage in it must always show deep mutual respect for one another's dignity and freedom.[4] To do this is always a challenge. It demands commitment, love, fidelity, and a sense of obligation and covenant. Commitments can be a source of joy, but also of tragedy, for, despite our best efforts, our commitments can break down.

---

3. This section presents and comments on Dworkin's argument in *Life's Dominion*, 68–84 (chapter 3, "What is Sacred?").

4. See Farley, *Just Love*, and *Personal Commitments*. By "just" Farley does not mean "only" love, but mutual respect for one another's dignity.

Some see the unique sacredness of human life as rooted in the capital importance of the preservation and prosperity of our own human species. They believe that, were humanity to disappear, all knowledge and culture would disappear. They see our species as the highest achievement of God's creation. In line with this way of thinking, Dworkin speaks of human life as a creative masterpiece, a triumph of "divine creation" or, secularly put, of natural evolutionary forces. As such, it is uniquely sacred. Even an immature embryo or fetus has all the DNA that destines and enables it to grow into a complex, reasoning human being.

All major Western religious traditions (Judaism, Christianity, and Islam) agree that God made humans in his own image or, as another biblical story has it, God breathed his divine breath into a piece of clay he had molded to give it life, thereby making it godlike.[5] From generation to generation evolutionary and reproductive processes produce new life from old life and bring forth ever-new forms of life and ever-new societal-cultural-political ways of living life. In traditionally religious terms, God is involved in the origin and evolution of all life.

Our awareness of the unique sacredness of human life is a powerful source for human compassion.[6] We are, and should be, horrified when human life is willfully and without reason destroyed. Its deliberate destruction dishonors what ought to be honored. Our horror reflects our shared, implicit sense of life's intrinsic importance and sacredness.[7]

5. Recall the two creation stories of Genesis analyzed in chapter 3.

6. We highlighted the notion of compassion in chapter 2 and then we discussed the three stories of origin and the four stories in Luke's Gospel that portrayed Jesus as a "person for others."

7. Despite our well-shared beliefs in the sacredness of life, many (in horrendously ironic ways) support the death penalty; decades, even lifelong, solitary confinement of prisoners; and sometimes even torture—all of which destroy human life in various ways. At the same time, these same people (again ironically) want death-row killings carried out with as little pain as possible and in ways that enable the victim to die within seconds. The same is true in

C. Dworkin's Position on the Morality of Abortion; For Clarity of Exposition We Present Dworkin's Position in Three Units

Unit (1): Life's Natural Progression: From Natural Biological Life (zoe) to Lived Life (bios)[8] To understand Dworkin's argument, it is helpful to know how he sees the natural progression (course) of human life. It begins with the biological conception of the embryo, continues through fetal development and the shock of birth, followed by infancy, childhood, adolescence, on to adulthood, and, hopefully, a long old age with a natural death.

Once born, a human begins to move beyond the mere natural, biological, physical investment in life (*zoe*) made by God, or, secularly put, by natural forces, to the personal, creative contributions and investments made by people, on their own initiative, for the development of their life (*bios*).[9] These personal contributions and investments are made in response to the challenges and opportunities which life presents and by making use of such gifts as the talents, intelligence, natural determination, initiative, imagination, ambition, creativity, physical gifts, emotional strengths, courage, and other gifts one is born with. Of course, each person is born with various kinds, numbers, and degrees of such gifts.

In deciding on an abortion, a woman should weigh all the factors involved: all the values and disvalues and all the options

---

the case of supporting weapons of mass destruction (nuclear, chemical, and biological).

The late Cardinal Joseph L. Bernardin recognized these inconsistencies and fought against them vigorously for many years, but with very limited success. See his book, *Seamless Garment*. He was much criticized by some pro-life advocates for putting the pro-life abortion position on par with other life issues, such as the death penalty, prison reform, the need for much better welfare programs, etc.

8. Dworkin, *Life's Dominion*, 88–94.

9. Dworkin uses the ancient Greek words *zoe* and *bios* in explaining his distinction between these two aspects of life.

and nonoptions. We saw this in the last chapter where we presented Gustafson's case study on abortion. Weighing these factors presents a problem. We humans are finite and, as we explained in chapter 2, do not have absolutely absolute guidelines that tell one how to weigh all the factors one should consider in making an abortion decision (or any other decision). So, each woman has to make her own value judgments about what is the most responsible and accountable thing to do. We stress that the woman alone has the right to make the final, definitive say whether to get or not get an abortion, for it is her body that is involved.

Equally important for one's personal, creative development are the opportunities (many a matter of birth and luck) that one has (or does not have) for education and individual social and cultural formation. These enable (or hinder) people to better develop the gifts they are born with and to take advantage of the opportunities that come their way. Thereby, they create further opportunities of their own making. People hope that their personal creative choices and responses will lead to ever more satisfying achievements, relationships, self-realizations, and self-fulfillments.

But both one's own natural, biological, and personal creative progression through life and the natural gifts one is born with can be blocked, frustrated, wrecked, or otherwise left unrealized. The worst possible is, of course, a premature death, but many other factors can also block them. Such factors include: poverty, sheer bad luck, tragic accidents that result in permanent mental or physical handicaps, and one's own misconceived projects and irreversible mistakes. All these can waste, frustrate, or wreck a person's efforts to live a full and flourishing life.

Unit (2): People's Convictions about Life and Its Degrees of Sacredness. In reading this unit, the reader should keep in mind Dworkin's conviction that every abortion is tragic, bad, and ethically problematic, though sometimes justifiable. The notion of degrees of sacredness is essential for understanding when he might see an abortion as "justifiable."

Dworkin holds that most conservatives and liberals accept the principle that human life is uniquely sacred, as explained in the previous section "B" of this chapter. Since abortion always wastes a human life, it is always in itself bad. Also conservatives and liberals generally agree that there are degrees of sacredness. What they disagree on is how to measure the degree of sacredness; that is, the relative importance of the various factors that a woman should weigh in deciding whether an abortion is justifiable in a given situation.

In the last chapter, we saw that even the official Catholic position allows a pregnant woman with a cancerous womb to choose to save her own life at the expense of her fetus' life by having a cancerous womb or section of the fallopian tube removed. The wasting of an embryo or fetus in such situations is certainly bad and tragic but still justifiable. It also means that the woman's life is regarded as having a greater degree of sacredness than that of the embryo or fetus.

For clarity, we now give some concrete examples that illustrate what Dworkin speaks of as "degrees" of sacredness. He does this not by "rationally proving this point (which is impossible) but by looking at how we spontaneously think about life.

For example, most people would agree (1) that it is worse when a young person dies in an airplane crash than when an elderly person does, for a younger person has a longer future ahead of her/him, which a premature death would wreck; (2) that it is worse when a teenager dies than a baby, for a teenager has made more of her/his life and gives more promise of future self-realizations than a baby, and so, if a teenager dies or suffers some tragic event, the teen would have more hopes and dreams "frustrated" than would a baby; (3) that when there is a scarcity of lifesaving medical resources, such as for a heart transplant, preference should be given to a parent of six underage children

Compassion and Respect

rather than to a bachelor or a mentally impaired person; (4) that when a woman experiences a late-term abortion (whether spontaneous or induced) it is not just emotionally more difficult but also a worse insult to the sacredness of human life than an early-term one; (5) that in war the lives of one's enemies are less sacred than those of one's own nation; (6) that it is sadder when a child or young person becomes severely handicapped for life by an accident than when an elderly person becomes handicapped.

These examples take into account both the chronological length of a life as well as its quality. By quality Dworkin means not only the personal, creative achievements, relationships, self-realizations, and self-fulfillments that a person has already achieved but also the promising potential achievements and self-realizations that a person and society hope and expect the person to achieve. A premature death or other factors mentioned above can frustrate (put an end to or limit) such potentials.

One's self-realizations include not just those that directly benefit oneself individually. They also include what a person has already contributed to the good of others and to society at large as well as the good that others and society at large expect the person to contribute in the future. Clear examples would include parents of young children, successful businesspersons with a good number of employees, musical geniuses, highly skilled surgeons, and scientists. Such people benefit not only themselves but also society at large. A premature death or other negative factor would frustrate not only the individual person but also others in society and society at large.

For Dworkin, all we have discussed here helps to explain why people, even without explicitly thinking about it, regard some lives as more sacred and important than others. That is, they implicitly believe there are degrees of sacredness. Why should this not apply also in the case of a woman whose pregnancy, if carried to term, may impact, for better or worse, either her life or the lives of others?

The problem is, how should a woman weigh all the values and disvalues and all the options and nonoptions that should be considered when she is faced with an abortion decision? (Again, recall all the factors and values Gustafson discusses in his case study in the previous chapter 5.)

Many conservatives believe that natural law or some God-given revelation will lead them to make the right judgments. But there are no rational proofs for such convictions. It comes down to a matter of faith and personal conviction.

Unit (3): The Conservative to Liberal Spectrum of Views on Abortion. Here we examine Dworkin's discussion of the range of views on the conservative to liberal spectrum.[10] He argues that few conservatives or liberals base their positions on abortion on personhood or the notion of the rights or interests of the embryo or fetus. (As we have noted, even the Vatican Congregation of the Faith acknowledges that science cannot establish that an embryo or fetus is a person.[11]) As Dworkin sees it, both conservatives and liberal base their argument, at least ultimately and implicitly, on the unique sanctity of all human life.

Conservatives. For them the natural, biological (or if you will, divine) contribution to human life (*zoe*) is almost everything. The very conservative give essentially no weight to the personal investments and contributions people make to their lives on their own initiatives (*bios*). Nor do they consider the effect that carrying a pregnancy to term may have on the mother or others that may be involved in raising the child.

For that reason, many conservatives believe that abortion is never, or at least very rarely, justifiable. But there are nuanced

---

10. Dworkin, *Life's Dominion*, 30–32 and 94–101 (conservative exceptions;); 32–35 and 94–101 (liberal exceptions.)

11. Cahill, "Catholic Perspective," 39.

exceptions. The most common are those where the mother's life is at stake or the pregnancy is the result of rape or forced incest.

They see rape and forced incest as "brutal" violations of divine law and an insult to the unique, God-given sacredness of a woman. For them rape and forced incest reduce a woman to a genital convenience, to someone whose love and sense of self have no significance. Forcing a woman to bear a child so conceived is a horrible, destructive assault on her human dignity. Rape and forced incest also frustrate the woman's creative freedom and ability for self-realization by preventing her from making her own reproduction decision. They grossly offend the sanctity of her life by forcing her to make "so-called love" against her will. A woman should not be made to pay for such brutal violations of her body and life by being forced to bring such a pregnancy to term.

On the other hand, and perhaps surprising to many, some conservatives believe there should be no laws forbidding abortion or contraception. They see abortion as a very personal, private matter rooted in deeply held religious convictions. So, especially in a society that recognizes the separation of church and state and guarantees freedom of religion, a woman should be free to make her own decision without any state interference, except perhaps for a very late-term abortion.[12] This would seem to put them on the very liberal end of the conservative-to-liberal spectrum,

However, many conservatives are not so tolerant. Many believe that the government should ban all abortions. Even a pregnancy that results from rape and forced incest leads such conservatives to sometimes ask: "Why should an embryo or fetus be made to forfeit its right to life and pay with its life for the wrongdoing of someone else?"

12. On this point, Dworkin cites a speech given at Notre Dame University by Roman Catholic former New York governor, Mario Cuomo, upholding this position (see Dworkin, *Life's Dominion*, 31, 145n1; Cuomo, "Religious Belief and Public Morality: A Catholic Governor's Perspective").

Liberals.[13] In speaking of liberals Dworkin excludes those who hold that abortion is not even an ethical issue. Like conservatives, the liberals Dworkin is thinking of accept the thesis that human life has a unique sacredness. For that reason, every abortion is tragic, bad, and ethically problematic, though at times justifiable.

Dworkin sees most liberals as primarily concerned with the personal investments and contributions persons make to their life (*bios*). They do not want them frustrated. Liberals are also concerned about *all* lives; they do not want anyone's life frustrated if a pregnancy is carried to term, whether it be that of the embryo, fetus, mother, or others in her family. Of course, in many cases this may be impossible; so someone's life may have to be compromised. Again, these decisions require value judgments on the part of the pregnant woman, for which there are no absolute guidelines.

Dworkin's Liberal Paradigm. To explain liberal views on abortion Dworkin presents his own paradigm of their position, though in doing so he is not suggesting that all liberals would fully agree with it. The paradigm has four elements.

First element. Abortion is a grave moral decision, especially from the moment an embryo successfully implants in the mother's placenta with its own distinctive DNA genetic individuality.[14] This normally occurs about fourteen days after the completion of fertilization. From that period on an embryo can no longer divide into two or more embryos, nor can two embryos combine to form one.

From that moment on, Dworkin holds, there can be no question that the deliberate extinction of the fetus represents a serious moral cost because of its unique, individualized sacredness. At least from that point on, an abortion is always more ethically problematic and tragic, even though in some

---

13. Dworkin, *Life's Dominion*, 32–34, 97–101.
14. Dworkin, *Life's Dominion*, 32–33.

situations justifiable. For this reason, its life must never be intentionally extinguished for any "trivial or frivolous reason." Dworkin gives three examples of what he means by "trivial" and "frivolous": (1) the woman wants to go on a long-awaited trip to Europe; or (2) she would prefer to be pregnant at a different time of the year; or (3) she has learned that her child would be a boy when she wanted a girl.

Second element. An abortion may be justifiable if it has been determined that the fetus has a serious abnormality and so, if born, the child can be expected to have a painful, frustrating, cruelly crippled, and often brief life.[15] In such cases an abortion may at times even be obligatory; for instance, it would be morally wrong for a woman to knowingly bring a child into the world if she has serious doubts about her capacity (what we speak of as emotional, physical, or economic wherewithal or strength) or the capacity of others involved in raising it to care for the child in an adequate way. The Kaveny's case study in the previous chapter is a good, concrete example. Of course, in that case the mother was never confronted with an abortion decision since she did not know that her fetus was seriously incapacitated.

Third element. This element raises the most challenging and difficult cases for justifying an abortion because it deals with a woman's own long-term personal, though deeply felt, interests or those of others in her family. The Gustafson case study analyzed in the previous chapter is a real-life example of such a case. The woman, pregnant because of a rape, had to make a troubling moral decision for which there was no clear-cut and seemingly compassionate answer.

In such cases, the woman is ultimately, and often unavoidably, left alone to discern her decision in the most responsible

---

15. In the next subsection we give examples of real-life cases where even children with the very severe handicaps have found love and have avoided serious frustration.

and accountable way she can. Such cases require a careful analysis of the whole situation. They may include, as we saw when discussing Gustafson's case study, cases like that of a teenager or an older woman who already has a large family. In today's societies, rarely is a teenager prepared either emotionally or economically to raise a child; the same may be the case with an older woman already with a large family, as Gustafson also noted.

Another example might be a mother and family who would not be able to afford to give her child the opportunities they want for the child or the child would be born into deep poverty in a society where welfare programs are very parsimonious and those born into poverty, though perhaps pitied, are looked down upon.[16]

Liberals who support these kinds of exceptions often assume that a woman who decides to have an abortion in such a case, would suffer some sadness and regret, but they would not condemn her decision. In some situations, liberals may even think that if the woman did not decide to have an abortion, she may have made a poor decision from a moral perspective.

Fourth element. Dworkin speaks of this element as a political one: the state has no right to intervene even to prevent morally impermissible abortions because the woman alone has the right to decide when an abortion is morally justifiable. As we have seen, even some moral conservatives share this same view.

Dworkin believes that these four elements represent the convictions of many liberals. The liberal view is clearly inconsistent with any notion that a fetus is a person and has rights and interests of its own or that the state has a right, perhaps even a duty, to criminalize such abortions.

Two Groups of Liberals. Dworkin also distinguishes two groups of liberals. One group focuses primarily on the

---

16. For the parsimony of welfare in the United States as compared to that of Western Europe, see Alesina and Glaeser, *Fighting Poverty*

frustration of the child to be born; the second on the effect a newborn child might have on those who must raise it.

The first group of liberals are most concerned about the frustration of the child to be born. This group sees abortion as possibly justifiable if the fetus is found to have a very grave physical or mental deformity that, if born, would make its life deprived, painful, stunted, and often very short. Kaveny's real-life case study of the Down Syndrome child is a case in point.

However, Dworkin is emphatic that it is not inevitable that a deformed child or one born into poverty will live a frustrated life or that it will frustrate the lives of others. After birth some seriously incapacitated children can and often do live quite enriched lives. They also can enrich the lives of those who lovingly care for them.

Also, some terribly handicapped children are born with the wherewithal (the determination and significant capacity to make use of it) that allows them to struggle and, to some degree, deal with, and even partially overcome their handicaps. Such children experience a profound satisfaction for what they managed to achieve and, additionally, richly reward those raising them.[17] (See the last section of this chapter for examples.)

The second group of liberals are most concerned with the frustration of those who must care for the child. They focus on how much the fetus, if born, may frustrate the life of the mother or the lives of others involved in raising the child. They see an abortion as possibly justifiable if a child is to be born into a family already overcome with other problems and do not feel they have the emotion or physical wherewithal to cope with raising a child or a additional child, either emotionally, physically, or financially. In this case, a new child might frustrate the life goals of those raising it. Again, in making such a decision, finite humans, especially pregnant women, are left to figure out on their

---

17. Dworkin, *Life's Dominion*, 97–98.

own how to weigh the values and options involved in the best responsible and accountable way they can.

Dworkin would not, at least necessarily and in all cases, accept this position: For many very poor, even single-parent mothers, children are the love of their lives. Raising a child is what gets them through life, though this should not be understood as the mother being motivated by her own selfish interests. For, the children of such very poor women feel the intense love their mother has for them and their lives are enhanced by it and they return their mother's profound love a hundredfold.[18]

Liberals who think this way, Dworkin observes, are also more likely than conservatives to support social legislation By social legislation, Dworkin means government-supported and promoted health care, homeschooling, child daycare, school meals, and programs for children with special needs (e.g., those with autism or hyperactive syndrome).

D. Real-life Examples of Handicapped Children Who Have Coped

In this section we examine some real-life cases that the author of this book is familiar with. They suggest that a pregnant woman who knows that her fetus, if born, will be severely handicapped should not automatically assume that she should have an abortion.

The author worked in Central America for nine years and became a close friend of a poor Salvadoran family. Eleven family members, spanning three generations, still live in a one-floor, cinderblock house with a corrugated metal roof. Like many poor Salvadoran families, they are very close-knit. The mother never had the chance to learn to read or write, but she raised all

---

18. For very scholarly case studies of how children born even into the deepest poverty have not been severely frustrated because of the immense love they receive and return, see Pimpare, *People's History of Poverty*, 113–140 (chapter 3, entitled "Love, Women Children).

her children to have tremendous initiative; her grandchildren also have tremendous get-up-and-go. They are also blessed with intelligence. Three of her nieces have gotten or are getting a university education thanks to the generosity of an uncle in the United States.

One of her daughters gave birth to a boy born with a rare and very severe form of epilepsy. He was expected to have a very short life, but he is now fourteen, however with the emotions and mind of a four-year-old.

The child's life is certainly deprived and stunted, and somewhat frustrated, but not completely so. He feels the love of his mother and his extended family and is enriched by it; he, in turn, enriches them through the love he feels and returns, though that love is that of a retarded four-year old.

But we should not deceive ourselves. Not every family structure has the needed wherewithal (ability) to give such a child the loving care s/he needs. We saw the importance of wherewithal in Kaveny's story of the child born with Down syndrome and the great tragedy that occurred because her mother did not have the wherewithal to deal with the child's tragic condition.

The author is a good friend of a family with five children (now grownup). The youngest are twins with significant mental retardation. The parents had the parenting skills as well as the financial means to make sure the twins would grow up to be independent. Each twin has been able to buy their own home.

One worked as a janitor most of his life. Early on he had the good fortune of falling in love with and marrying a registered nurse who had graduated from an Ivy League university. This son and his wife had six children, all in good heath and now mostly grown up. They love one another dearly.

The other twin has always worked as a hospital orderly. Many of the patients he has cared for have been effusive in praise of him for his cheerful attitude.

Again, we should not deceive ourselves. Not all parents are blessed with the financial means and parenting skills the twins' parents had.

The author recently saw two TV human interest stories. One was about a preschool boy who was born with an incomplete spinal cord. Physicians said he would never walk. But he was born with tremendous determination and drive, as well as otherwise good health. Somehow, he learned to crawl. He can now take some struggling steps with the help of a walker to stand up.

Another recent TV story interviewed a six-year-old boy born without hands, though his right arm did seem to have a little stub on it, perhaps the size of one joint of a child's little finger. He had just won a citywide cursive handwriting contest. TV news showed him beautifully writing something but it was impossible to see on TV how he was able to hold the pencil.

Again, we should not deceive ourselves; not everyone has such determination or the ability to figure out how to do something that seems impossible.

Chapter 7

Family Planning, Personhood, and Human Reproduction (IVF)

This chapter has three sections, A through C.

A. The Importance of Family Planning and Contraception for Avoiding Unwanted Pregnancies

B. Personhood, Human Individuality, and Embryology Science

C. Human Reproduction: In-Vitro Fertilization (IVF)

A. The Importance of Family Planning and Contraception for Avoiding Unwanted Pregnancies

If we are to reduce the number of abortions, we have to think about family planning; that also means contraception. At least since the mid-twentieth century, medical scientists have used their natural (god-given) intelligence to develop contraceptive medicines and devices that when properly used are quite effective in preventing unwanted conceptions, though none is always effective.

There are many ethically responsible and compassionate reasons why women and men should make use of them. These reasons include economic ones as well as the emotional and physical health of the woman, her partner, and others who may help care for the child. They also include judgments of whether they want to have or not have a child and, if so, when, how many, and what opportunities in life the parents (or parent) wishes to give their child.

If a couple do not wish to conceive a child but want to engage in genital sex, they should use the best contraceptive methods (devices or medicines) available. To do otherwise would be ethically irresponsible, for everything possible should be done to avoid an unwanted pregnancy and a need to consider abortion. As Dworkin argues, every abortion is tragic and ethically problematic, even if at times justifiable. For the poor, family planning counselling and contraceptives should be readily available through governmental and non-profit organizations.

Some pro-life advocates and religious groups condemn contraception as unnatural. We have already indicated why we consider it quite natural that humans use their intelligence to aid in family planning. As to "thwarting the primary end of genital sex," essentially everyone, including psychologists, psychiatrists, sociologists, and religious groups recognize that genital sex serves many noble ends besides that of producing children. These ends include strengthening a couple's bonds of love in ways that go well beyond what can be done through just kisses and hugs.

Moreover, couples commit themselves to a hopefully lasting relationship for various reasons. Some do so without any desire to produce or raise children. Their primary, and only goal, is to mutually support one another in their life's goals, for example, in their professional careers. Others enter such relationships even though they know they can never produce a child because they are sterile or because the woman is beyond the childbearing age. Still others engage in genital sex but want to postpone having children for one reason or another.

Family Planning, Personhood, and Human Reproduction (IVF)

No religious group prohibits couples from entering marital relationships for such reasons as these.

Birth Control Methods.[1] There are about seventeen birth control methods. One is the rhythm method, which is the only one officially permitted by the Roman Catholic Church. This method requires a woman to make a careful calculation each month to determine on what days of the month she is likely to be fertile. To be sure she does not get pregnant, she must do her best to have intercourse only on days she is fairly sure she is not fertile. To do so she must calculate what day she expects to begin her next period. This is difficult because many factors not under her control can cause her period to vary from month to month. Because of this uncertainty, many pejoratively speak of the rhythm method as Russian roulette.

In the last seventy years or so medical science has developed numerous other contraceptive methods. None of these methods works if a pregnancy has already begun. If a sperm has already entered an egg, no contraceptive can abort an already fertilized egg or one in the process of being fertilized. All contraceptive methods function only to prevent a conception; none can end it. However, no contraceptive method is 100 percent effective.

Women and men should consider several factors to determine which are the most appropriate method or methods for them. Among the factors are their safety, effectiveness, accessibility, affordability, personal preference, and medical acceptability. A woman would do well to consult with her gynecologist

---

1. Centers For Disease Control and Prevention, "Contraception." This is the most exhaustive wesite that explains methods of contraception. It also provides images of many of the contraceptive devices it discusses. Also see American College of Obstetricians and Gynecologists (ACOG), "ACOG Statement on Abortion Bans," and Centers for Disease Control and Prevention, "Effectiveness of Family Planning Methods." https://www.cdcgov/reproductvehealth/unintendedpregnancy/pdf//contraceptive_methods_506.pdf. Accessed August 14, 2020.

about the various methods and what are best for her, especially if she wishes to make regular use of them.

In choosing a method it is wise that both the woman and the man keep in mind protection from HIV and other STDs.[2] Some contraceptive methods, not all, afford some protection against these diseases. We will not go into HIV and other STDs here.

Consistent and correct use of any contraceptive method is important. This means never failing to use them every time a couple has sex. If that is not possible in some situation, they should have second thoughts about having sex at that time. Some methods require the assistance of a gynecologist. We describe each. Should a woman wish to conceive, she can simply cease to make use of them.

Spermicide, for both women and men. It works by killing sperm before any make contact with an egg. It is available in several forms: foam, gel, cream, film, suppository, and tablet. (For greater protection spermicide should be used along with other contraceptive methods.) In applying it, a woman needs to be careful to coat well her entire vagina area no more than one hour before intercourse and leave the spermicide in place for at least six to eight hours after intercourse. Some male condoms come coated with spermicide, but the coating is often not enough. Spermicide is available over the counter at drug stores.

Intrauterine Devices (IUD): two types, both for women. Each is a "T" shaped device and must be inserted inside the uterus by a gynecologist. They can be left in place for up to five or ten years and so give long-term protection. They seek to prevent sperm from entering an egg, but like all contraceptive methods, neither is always effective. A gynecologist can remove the device any time a woman wishes.

---

2. HIV stands for Human Immunodeficiency Virus. This virus attacks the body's immune system by destroying CD4 cells and can lead to Acquired Immune Deficiency Syndrome (AIDS). STDs refer to all sexually transmittable diseases.

Hormonal Methods: Six types, all for women. They work by releasing progestin into the woman's body in an effort to prevent a pregnancy. One is a simple thin rod of progestin that a physician inserts under the skin of the woman's arm. It can work for as many as three years before having to be replaced, but it may be removed earlier. The second is an injection shot that a gynecologist gives a woman in her buttocks or arm every three months. So both give short-term protection. Again, like all contraceptive methods, neither is always effective.

Two others are hormone pills that contain progestin and estrogen. All must be prescribed by a physician. One or other must be taken at the same time each day. The fifth hormone method is a skin patch a woman puts on her lower abdomen, buttocks, or upper body (but not on her breasts). It can be worn for three weeks before needing replacement. Again, like all contraceptive methods, none is always effective.

The final hormonal type is a vaginal contraceptive ring which releases progestin and estrogen. The woman herself places it inside her vagina, but she should consult her gynecologist to be sure she knows how to insert it properly. She can wear it for three weeks but then it should be taken out for a week so she can have a period. Then she can insert a new ring. Like all contraceptive methods, it is not always effective.

Barrier Methods: five types, four for women, one for men. They function by blocking semen from entering an egg. Two (for women) are the diaphragm and the cervical cap. They come in several sizes. So the woman needs to have her gynecologist determine the right size and show her how to insert it properly. Once she knows how, the woman herself can place either inside her vagina. Both cover the cervix and block sperm from fertilizing an egg. The diaphragm is a shallow cup. The cervical cap is a thimble-shaped cup. Before sexual intercourse, the woman must carefully insert one or other, along with spermicide, to cover her cervix. Each of these methods seek to block or kill any sperm that seeks to enter her fallopian tube. Neither is designed to be left in permanently.

The third barrier type is the contraceptive sponge. It contains spermicide. The woman herself places it in her vagina so that it fits over and well covers the entire cervix. The sponge works for up to 24 hours and must be left in the vagina for at least six hours after intercourse, at which time it must be removed and discarded. It is advisable that the woman check with her physician to be sure she knows how to insert it properly. It is available over the counter at drug stores. Like all contraceptive methods, neither is always effective.

The final two, the female and male condom, help to prevent sperm from getting into the woman's body. They should not be used together since their latex-like material can easily dislodge one another.

The female condom usually comes with a lubricant and is available at drug stores. It can be inserted up to eight hours before intercourse and is best used with a spermicide. Male condoms keep the man's sperm from getting into a woman's body. Some come with spermicide or water-based lubricants. The most common type is made of latex. They help to prevent a pregnancy but may not provide protection against STD (sexually transmittable diseases). Condoms can be used only once. They are readily available at drug stores.

The male condom is the most effective of all contraceptive devices, much more so than the female condom. The male condom comes rolled up. Once the male has his erection, he unrolls it down his erect penis so that it covers it completely. Condoms should not be used with oil-based lubricants since they can weaken the condom's wall, causing it to tear or break. After climaxing, a man should be careful in removing the condom so that no sperm seeps into the woman's vagina.

Emergency contraception pill, for women.[3] A woman should not use this pill as a regular form of birth control. This pill is commonly known as the morning-after pill; it is medically known as Levonorgestrel. It is a progestin, a hormone that is used in many birth control pills. Women use it to prevent a pregnancy after a birth control failure (such as a broken condom) or unprotected sex. It works mainly by preventing the release of an egg (ovulation) during a woman's menstrual cycle. It also thickens her vaginal fluid; this, too, helps to prevent sperm from reaching an egg (and thus fertilizing it). Using this medication does not end an existing pregnancy; that is, it does not cause an abortion. Nor does it protect her or her partner against sexually transmitted diseases (STDs).

Levonorgestrel is sold under various names: Plan B One Step, Take Action, My Way, and AfterPill. The woman simply swallows the tablet the way she does any other pill. It can lower a woman's chance of getting pregnant from 70 to 89 percent. For maximum effectiveness, she should take it within three days after unprotected sex but she can take it up to five days, though this reduces its effectiveness. But no matter when it is taken, it is not guaranteed to stop a pregnancy from occurring.

For medical reasons, a woman should not take more than one tablet of levonorgestrel if she has taken one since her last period; nor would doing so provide her any extra protection from a pregnancy.

The morning-after pill is very safe; side effects are rare. The only significant side effects may be a feeling of nausea, lightheadedness, dizziness, or tenderness in her breasts for a short while. If she throws up within two hours after taking it, it won't work and so she should take another one; however, this is the only situation where she should take a second tablet.

After taking it, a woman should recognize that it is totally normal that her next period may be different from what she is

---

3. See "Emergency Contraception."

used to; that is, it may come earlier or later, or be heavier, or lighter, or be more spotty than before. However, her period may also remain the same as it has normally been.

The morning-after pill can be expensive. However, a woman may be able to get the morning-after pill free or at low cost from a Planned Parenthood health or other family planning clinic. Otherwise, it may cost as much as forty or fifty dollars, though a generic brand, called AfterPill, is also available online for about twenty dollars, plus five dollars shipping. Planned Parenthood may also help a woman to figure out if her health insurance will pay for it. In brief, a woman should shop around.

Permanent Methods of Birth Control. These are rather drastic measures because they are usually not reversible. There are two types, one for the woman, the other for the man. For the woman there is an operation called tubal ligation. It ties the fallopian tubes so that sperm and eggs cannot meet in it. This procedure can be done in a hospital or outpatient surgical center. She can go home the same day as the surgery and resume her normal activities within a few days. This method is effective immediately.

For the male there is an operation called a vasectomy. This operation keeps a man's sperm from ever going into his penis. He can still ejaculate but since his sperm never gets into the ejaculation it can never fertilize an egg. The procedure is typically done at an outpatient surgical center. The man can go home the same day. Recovery time is less than one week. However, it is generally not effective immediately. So about twelve weeks after the operation, the man must visit his doctor for tests to make sure his sperm count has dropped to zero. If a male want to have intercourse during this intervening period, he should use another form of birth control until he is certain that his sperm count has dropped to zero.

B. Personhood, Human Individuality, and Embryology Science[4]

Our focus here is on the inconsistencies between what embryology science has found and the pro-life argument for personhood from the moment of conception. Strictly speaking, the word "person" cannot be defined. The best we can do is to say that we know one when we see one.

In other words, it is like such words as "sunset" or "pain." We know it when we experience it. Thus, we instinctively know that a corpse is not a person but a crying baby is a person. At best we can only describe the characteristics we associate with a "person."

Examples of two such descriptive definitions are: (1) a person is a being that has certain capacities or attributes such as reason, morality, consciousness, or self-consciousness and is a part of a culturally established form of social relations, such as kinship, ownership of property, or legal responsibility; (2) a person is a being characterized by consciousness, rationality, and a moral sense, and traditionally thought of as consisting of both a body and a mind or soul.

Embryologists and geneticists recognize that an embryo and fetus have all the human DNA to become a "person" from the moment of conception. However, embryos and fetuses do not clearly start to develop the characteristics we associate with personhood until well into the second trimester. "Becoming" a person is a long, almost nine-month, process. Embryology science cannot determine when it occurs.

Observe, too, that, although many Christians speak of embryos and fetuses as persons from the moment of conception, Christian baptismal ritual does not provide for the baptism of spontaneously or otherwise aborted embryos and fetuses or of fetuses born already dead. So, it would seem that in the

---

4. For the medical science of this section, see Sadler, *Langman's Medical Embryology*, 10–62.

Christian baptismal tradition embryos and fetuses have not been considered "persons" with a soul to be saved.

Personhood and the Christian tradition.[5] Medieval Christian theologians, including Thomas Aquinas in the thirteenth century, did not employ the words "person" or "personhood." They did speak of "quickening" and "soul implantation." Quickening occurred when a pregnant woman first felt the fetus move in her womb. It was then that God was thought to have implanted a "soul" in the fetus.

Also, if an embryo or fetus was deliberately killed before quickening, for some centuries, the Christian theological tradition considered it only the lesser sin of murder rather than what was the much graver sin of abortion. Only much later did a Pope declare that killing an embryo or fetus at any time after conception was to be considered the more serious sin of abortion.

Embryonic science presents serious challenges to the "the-embryo-is-a-person" view. First, the fertilization of an egg is a "process," not a "moment." Once a sperm has made contact with an egg, it takes between twenty-four and forty-eight hours to complete the fertilization of an egg. (Nature does not permit more than one sperm to enter a given egg.) Fertilization takes place between the sixth and tenth day after intercourse, assuming that the woman does actually conceive.

Second, it takes up to fourteen days for a fertilized egg to implant in the mother's womb and it does not develop into a fetus until the placenta has been fully formed in the womb. The placenta needs time to develop because it is the placenta that allows for thermoregulation, gas exchange, and the passing of nutrients via the mother's blood supply to the fetus, all of which are necessary for fetal development.

Third, and most significantly, embryology has determined that up to fourteen days after conception a fertilized egg can

---

5. Cahill, "Catholic Perspective," 2009.

divide into two or more fertilized eggs (thus producing identical twins, triplets, etc.) and, though more rarely, if two eggs have been fertilized and implanted in the womb, they can unite and become only a single fertilized egg. If one considers a fertilized egg a "person," these scientific findings would seem to mean that a "single person" (one fertilized egg) can divide into two or more "persons" and that two "persons" (two fertilized eggs) can unite to become " a single person" (fertilized egg).

How do those who hold the embryo is a person-from-the moment-of-conception address these findings of embryonic science? The only attempt to answer these questions this writer is aware of was offered by the very traditional Roman Catholic lay philosopher Germain Grisez, in his book, *Abortion, the Myths, the Realities, and the Arguments*.[6]

To answer these questions, Grisez introduced the term "individual human life." Individual human life, Grisez argued, begins when an egg and sperm meet. This "meeting" produces a zygote with a full complement of forty-six chromosomes. So how does Grisez explain the phenomenon that one fertilized egg can divide into two or more fertilized eggs to produce identical twins, etc., and the phenomenon of two fertilized eggs can combining to become one?

In the case of twinning, he argued that we must think in terms of three "individual human lives," A, B, and C, *not* in terms of persons. "B" and "C" are two individual lives; they sprung from their grandparent "A." Grisez called this a form of "atypical reproduction," such as happens in many lower forms of life that can develop by the division of a single individual. Kaveny's response to this explanation is that from both Christian and scientific perspectives humans reproduce sexually, not "asexually."

---

6. We owe our reference to Grizez to Cathleen Kaveny, *Culture of Engagement*, 223–225. Germain Gabriel Grisez (1929 –2018) was a French-American lay Catholic philosopher. His ideas were rooted in Thomas Aquinas.

Grisez explained the phenomenon of two embryos uniting to form one by saying this involves two "individual human lives, *not* persons, that combine to form one individual life. This, Grisez wrote, is analogous to that of a grafted plant. The somewhat conservative twentieth-century Protestant moral theologian, Paul Ramsey, responded to Grisez's explanation by asking with astonishment "whether any such 'individuality' is the life we should respect and protect from the moment of conception?" In trying to prove too much, Ramsey said, "Grisez proved too little of ethical import."

For the author of this book, a far better explanation of individuality, and one more in accord with embryology science, has been offered by Ronald Dworkin.[7] From the moment of conception an embryo has all the DNA to develop into a human. However, it does not have a definitive "genetic individuality" because until about fourteen days after conception, a fertilized egg that has descended into the mother's womb can divide into two or more embryos; or if two fertilized eggs have descended into the womb, they can unite to form one fertilized egg. Only after this approximate fourteen-day period, does an embryo take on its own fixed genetic individuality with its own genetic DNA. In doing so, Dworkin argues, it takes on a higher degree of sacredness and any decision to terminate the pregnancy becomes graver and more morally problematic, though, at least for Dworkin, not necessarily unjustifiable. During this fourteen-day period a woman is usually unaware of her pregnancy and not even pregnancy tests can detect it. So, usually by the time she is aware of her pregnancy, the embryo (or embryos) has (have) already its attained genetic individuality.

---

7. Dworkin, *Life's Dominion*, 32–33.

FAMILY PLANNING, PERSONHOOD, AND HUMAN REPRODUCTION (IVF)

C. Human Reproduction: In-Vitro Fertilization (IVF)[8]

Our discussion of human reproduction is limited to in-vitro fertilization procedures because they are the only ones that have had any noteworthy, even though limited, success[9]

The word "in-vitro" is Latin for "in a dish." In-vitro fertilization means that a egg is fertilized with sperm in a laboratory dish rather than in one of the woman's fallopian tubes or in the uterus. IVF offers a number of complex, high-tech procedures that compassionately address various reproduction problems of both men and women. Most IVF procedures are carried out in specialized clinics not associated with a traditional hospital.

Some religious groups see IVF procedures as "unnatural" and prohibit their use. But most people see them as quite natural since scientists have developed them by using their "natural" (god-given) intellects to compassionately help those with human reproduction issues.

IVF involves taking eggs (by suction, a quite unpleasant procedure) from a woman's ovaries and fertilizing them with sperm (obtained by a man masturbating into a collection condom) in a laboratory. The sperm and eggs that are used can be that of the couple or that of a donor or a mix of the two. Sperm, eggs, and even embryos can also be kept in frozen storage for years and then defrosted as needed. It is now quite routine for anyone, including an adolescent who is to undergo chemotherapy or radiation therapy, to have some of their sperm or

8. The medical science for this section is based on Sher et al., *In Vitro Fertilization*; this book was not written for specialists but for anyone considering an IVF procedure. See also Mayo Clinic, "In-Vitro Fertilization (IVF)"; Society for Assisted Reproductive Technology, "What Is SART?" Se also see Sher et al., *In Vitro Fertilization*, 228–41.

9. At least in the United States there is a whole industry, sometimes referred to as "Femtech" (Fem = female), that seeks to develop technology to help those with reproduction problem. Except for IVF, their technologies have had very limited success. Often a procedure that works for one woman, doesn't work for others. For an excellent up-to-date account of this industry, see Allman, "Mommy and Daddy," 28–35.

eggs put in frozen storage. Some couples have embryos they produced in a IVF clinic kept in frozen storage because they do not want a child immediately for economic, medical, or professional career reasons but may wish to have a child later in life. However, frozen storage does not guarantee that any stored sperm, eggs, or embryos can be successfully used.

When a woman is to use her own eggs, often her gynecologist will medicate her for at least a month to ensure that the eggs collected are of the highest quality.[10] Some people donate eggs, sperm, and even embryos with the intention of selling them or simply giving them to persons who cannot produce their own child.

Embryos created in an IVF clinic are always tested and only the best is planted in a woman's womb so that she can, hopefully, bring forth a child within nine months. (IVF cannot develop fetuses; a fetus can develop only by being nurtured in a woman's womb.)

IVF procedures and the storage of frozen eggs, sperm, and embryos are very expensive (in the United States, thousands of dollars) and are not necessarily covered by health insurance. So it is not really available to many persons. (This, of course, raises a serious societal ethical issue since it is economically not available to many.) However, since the 1980s, at least fifteen states (Arkansas, California, Connecticut, Hawaii, Illinois, Louisiana, Maryland, Massachusetts, Montana, New Jersey, New York, Ohio, Rhode Island, Texas, and West Virginia) have passed laws requiring insurers to either cover or offer coverage for infertility diagnosis and treatment.

If the egg, sperm, or embryo of a third-party donor is used, the woman or couple receiving the IVF treatment will not bring forth a child that has a biological DNA wholly theirs or,

---

10. IVF came to the fore in 2018 when Micelle Obama reported in her book *Becoming* and on TV interviews that she and Barack had their two daughters with the help of an IVF procedure. In their case, they used their own sperm and eggs, and her eggs were enriched before being fertilized in the IVF laboratory.

FAMILY PLANNING, PERSONHOOD, AND HUMAN REPRODUCTION (IVF)

in some procedures, even half biologically theirs. However, it would have half their DNA if either the egg or sperm used came from one of the couple. Examples of some problems that IVF procedures can compassionately address are:

1. Some women have a problem conceiving a child even though they are fertile. *However, medical tests show she may be able to bring an implanted embryo to term.* She and her partner can have one of her eggs fertilized "in-vitro" with her partner's sperm and then have the resulting embryo implanted in her womb; she would then bring it to term. The child brought forth will have the couple's DNA. (This was the case with the Obamas.)

2. *If a woman has a sterile partner but is herself fertile and capable of bringing a child to term,* she could have some of her eggs fertilized "in-vitro" with the sperm of a donor, and then have the best resulting embryo implanted in her womb. She would bring it to term. The child would then have the biological DNA of the mother but not that of her male partner. However, the couple would raise the child as their own and her male partner would have effectively adopted the child from *before* birth (not just "at" birth). The adopting father would have the wonderful experience of supporting his partner throughout her pregnancy and will have already started emotionally bonding with his adopted, but still to be born, child.

3. *If a man has a sterile partner but his female partner is capable of bringing a child to term, he could fertilize "in-vitro" a donor egg.* The resulting embryo would be implanted in his partner's womb and she would bring it to term. Her male partner would be the biological father and she would be equivalently the adopting mother since she had brought the embryo to term and would have the wonderful experience of having provided the fetus all the nutrients it needed to develop properly. Though the child born would not have the mother's DNA, the couple would raise the child as their own.

There are a number of IVF procedures for addressing other reproduction issues. For example, some can enable a gay or lesbian person to raise a child that has half her/his DNA.

IVF Success Rate. Though by no means always successful, IVF procedures are essentially medically safe. IVF success rates depends on many factors: e.g., age, whether the woman had been able to have a previous pregnancy and whether it was with the same mate, etc. Also, the younger the woman is, the more likely she is to get pregnant and give birth to a healthy baby using her own eggs or those of another woman. Studies also indicate that donor eggs offer a better chance for success.

Ethical Objections to IVF. We consider two. The first has to do with the disposal of frozen stored eggs, sperm, embryos. Today, in the United States alone, there are millions of frozen eggs, sperm, and embryos in storage. Only a minuscule percentage of them will ever be actually used for IVF procedures. Such tissues do not last forever. So hundreds of thousands of them become useless after time and will need to be destroyed. From an ethical perspective, how might we think about their disposal (destruction)?

Some argue that no one objects to the storage of many types of human tissue for later use: for example, blood, hearts, kidneys, and limbs. It is a very compassionate thing to do. So why object to the storage and use of human reproductive tissues? They also are being stored for very compassionate reasons. Of course, their destruction should be done with appropriate reverence because of the unique sacredness of all human life.

The second ethical objection is that IVF is unnatural. It is true that its methods do not produce children in the ordinary way genital sex does. But, as we have noted elsewhere, there is nothing unnatural for humans to use their "god-given" intelligence to search for responsible and compassionate ways to help men and woman who cannot produce children through normal genital intercourse or for whom doing so in the ordinary way might be medically risky. Indeed, we humans were given intelligence to enable us to make for a better and more compassionate world and we have been doing so for many millennia.

Natural ways of losing reproductive tissue. Again, from an ethical perspective, how might we look upon the following:

First, in the case of eggs: when born a woman has approximately one to two million eggs in her ovaries. By puberty, only about 300,000 remain. Only about five hundred of these will be ovulated during the woman's reproductive lifetime. Thus, the vast majority of the eggs within her ovaries at her birth get steadily depleted (die out or somehow disappear) until they become completely depleted at menopause. Many are also lost in a woman's monthly periods. Thus, nature itself, or if you will, God, allows for the destruction and loss of hundreds of thousands of eggs.

Second in the case of *sperm*. Healthy men produce from 1.5 to 5 milliliters of semen each time they ejaculate.[11] Hundreds of millions of sperm are lost in nocturnal ejaculations. In genital sex millions of sperm die before they ever reach an egg and no more than one sperm can enter a egg to fertilize it. So, as with women's eggs, millions of sperm die or disappear.

Finally, in the case of *spontaneous miscarriages*, as we have indicated before, it is estimated that ten to twenty percent of known pregnancies end in miscarriages, mostly before the twentieth week of a pregnancy. However, the actual number is likely higher because many miscarriages occur so early in a pregnancy that a woman doesn't yet realize she's pregnant; nor is there any medical test that can detect a pregnancy in its earliest stage. Many embryologists think that many miscarriages occur because of fetal defects in the embryos or fetuses. Whatever is the case, we can say that miscarriages of defective embryos and fetuses are nature's (or if you will, God's) way of disposing of them before they are born.

---

11. See Mayo Clinic, "Low Sperm Count."

CHAPTER 8

Public Policy Discourse
A Real-life Example

THE 2015 SUPREME COURT ruling on same-sex marriage is an excellent real-life example of how to carry on public policy discourse and decision-making in a secular, pluralistic world. It dealt with a very divisive issue. We make it the subject of our conclusion because the way in which the five majority ruling justices went about making their decision is similar to the way we do ethics in this book and to the kind of respectful, compassionate discourse we seek to foster in this book. For these reasons, the ruling makes for a good concluding chapter for this book. It has eight sections, A through H:

A. Introduction

B. How the Issue Came Before the US Supreme Court

C. The Supreme Court Ruling as Public Policy Discourse

D. The Supreme Court Ruling as Societal Justice Analysis

E. The Court's Ruling as Searching for a Mediating Middle Ground

F. The Court's Decision as a Compassionate, Respectful Search for and Finding a Nonjudgmental Mediating Middle Ground

G. The Importance of Married Love for Society and Individuals

H. The Court's Decision as Compassionate, Respectful, and Non-judgmental Interpretation of Law

A. Introduction

The Supreme court ruling on same-sex marriage is an excellent real-life example in four respects: (1) public policy discourse and analysis at its best in a secular, pluralistic world; (2) societal justice analysis; (3) searching for and finding a mediating, middle ground on an important but very divisive public policy issue; and (4) compassionate, respectful, nonjudgmental interpretation of law.

The ruling was a narrow five to four one. The four dissenting justices felt so strongly about their dissents that each wrote their own separate brief in response to the majority ruling. We do not examine the dissenting briefs for they focus primarily on legal aspects of the case. Our interest is in the ethical aspects.

In their ruling, the five concurring majority justices began by stating certain basic notions that undergirded their decision. The two that interests us most are (1) the right of personal choice as inherent in the notion of individual autonomy and (2) the uniqueness and societal importance, for society as well as for individuals, of the love commitment that two persons make when entering into the conjugal union of marriage, whether it be heterosexual or same-sexual.

B. How the Issue Came Before the US Supreme Court

Fourteen plaintifs (also called petitioners or appellants) from the states of Kentucky, Michigan, Ohio, and Tennessee had challenged their respective state laws on marriage in four different federal district courts. These laws defined marriage as a union between one man and one woman and accordingly issued marriage licenses only to heterosexual couples. Also these state laws did not recognize same-sex marriages legally performed in other states. The plaintiffs' argument was that their state laws violated their fourteenth amendment rights because they denied them their federal Constitutional rights of equal protection under the law.

The four lower federal district courts had ruled in favor of the plaintiffs by declaring the law of each of their states unconstitutional under the fourteenth Amendment of the US Constitution. The rulings of these lower federal courts meant that those four states could not deny a same-sex couple a marriage license or refuse to recognize a same-sex marriage performed in another state.

However, the attorney generals of the four states appealed the four lower district court rulings to the Sixth Circuit Federal Appeals Court to reverse the lower federal courts rulings. After consolidating the four lower court rulings, this federal appeals court reversed the four lower court rulings, thereby declaring that the fourteenth amendment of the US Constitution did not oblige states to issue marriage licenses to same-sex couples or to recognize same-sex marriages legally performed in other states.

So, the fourteen plaintiffs appealed the Sixth Federal Circuit Appeal Court ruling to the US Supreme Court. They asked the Supreme Court to reverse the ruling the Sixth Federal Circuit Appeal Court and reinstate the rulings of the four lower Federal District Courts. In reply, the responders (the four state officials responsible for enforcing the laws of their states) asked the Supreme Court to deny the plaintiffs' petition and uphold the ruling of the Federal Circuit Appeal Court and, thereby, uphold the constitutionality of the state laws.

C. The Supreme Court Ruling as Public Policy Discourse

To be most effective, public policy discourse in a secular, pluralistic, divided society, like that of the United States, requires as widespread and as diverse "public" participation as possible. The five-to-four Supreme Court ruling had such participation. Of course, like the four dissenting justices, many citizens will not agree with the Supreme Court's ruling but hopefully most can live with it. Our argument is as follows.

First, besides the nine Supreme Court justices, the fourteen plaintiffs and their attorneys, the four state responders, and a number of lower court rulings (in legalese known as "case law"), the Supreme Court also received well over a hundred "*amici curiae*" (friends of the Court) briefs on the case.

The *amici curiae* briefs represented a wide variety of essentially all the central institutions in American life. For example, they included briefs from state and local governments, the military, large and small businesses, labor unions, religious organizations, law enforcement and civic groups, professional organizations, and universities. All this quite diverse democratic input demonstrates widespread public participation in the case, It also substantially enhanced the US Supreme Court's understanding of the issue and is reflected in the majority Court's ruling.

Second, the Supreme Court considered the question of whether it should await further state and federal legislation, litigation, debate, and study before accepting and ruling on the case. The majority's response to this question was: (1) that there already had been extensive legislation, litigation, grassroots activism campaigns, and studies of the issue; and (2) that, given long, widespread public discussion and the nature of our pluralistic democracy and its commitment to individual liberty and freedom of religion, persons who felt harmed by same-sex marriage restriction (like the fourteen plaintiffs) ought not to have to await further public input and legislative action.

Third, in the ruling the five concurring Supreme Court Justices also noted that in recent years other lower federal district courts had written a substantial body of law (called "case law") that considered all sides of the same-sex issue. Moreover, except for the decision of the Sixth Circuit Federal Appeal Court (the one that the Supreme Court was now reviewing) and one other lower federal district circuit court ruling, various other lower federal district courts had examined the issue and had ruled that excluding same-sex couples from marriage was unconstitutional.

D. The Supreme Court Ruling as Societal Justice Analysis[1]

The five justices in the majority did what we speak of as societal justice analysis. First, they considered the significance and urgency of a decision from the perspective of the plaintiffs. As examples, it briefly narrated in its ruling the situations of five of the plaintiffs.

Co-plaintiff James Obergefell was from Ohio. He had met his same-sex partner, John Arthur, over two decades ago. They fell in love and started living together, However, in 2011 John Arthur was diagnosed with ALS disease. Two years later James and John decided to make an everlasting commitment to one another and resolved to marry before John Arthur died. To fulfill their mutual promises, they traveled from Ohio (where same-sex marriage was not recognized) to Maryland (where same-sex marriage was legal). It was difficult for John Arthur to move, so they hired a medical transport plane. After it landed in Baltimore but while still on the tarmac, they legally wedded inside the plane.

---

1. The ruling did not use the term "societal justice analysis," but that is what it was.

Three months later John Arthur died. However, the laws of his home state of Ohio did not permit James Obergefell to be listed as the surviving spouse on John Arthur's death certificate. So, as James Obergefell saw and experienced it, by state statute he and his same-sex partner would remain strangers even in death. James Obergefell found this "hurtful" and brought suit in Ohio to demand that he be listed as the surviving spouse on Arthur's death certificate. A federal district court ruled in his favor. But the state of Ohio appealed to the Sixth Circuit Federal Appeals Court which reversed the lower district court's decision. So James Obergefell join in on the appeal made to the US Supreme Court to overturn the ruling of the Sixth Circuit Appeals Court.

Co-plaintiffs April DeBoer and Jayne Rowse were from Michigan. Both were nurses. They celebrated a commitment ceremony to honor their permanent relation in 2007. In 2009, Michigan law allowed DeBoer and Rowse to foster, then adopt, a baby boy, but recognized only one partner as the legal adopting parent, for Michigan law permitted only opposite-sex married couples or single women to adopt. So the state of Michigan considered only one of this same-sex couple as the legal adopting parent. Later that same year, April and Jayne welcomed another son into their family. The new baby, born prematurely and abandoned by the biological mother, required around-the-clock care. The next year, a baby girl with special needs also joined their family. (No couple could be more pledged to making for a better world than April and Jayne.)

But if an emergency arose, Michigan schools and hospitals would have to treat the three children as if they had only one parent. If a tragedy were to befall either DeBoer or Rowse, it would be uncertain whether the surviving one would have legal parental rights over the children. For this reason, the couple appealed to the Supreme Court in the hope of finding relief from the uncertainty in their lives because Michigan State recognized only one of then as the adopting parent.[2]

Co-plaintiffs Army Reserve Sergeant Ijpe (sic) *DeKoe and Thomas Kostura* were from Tennessee. They had fallen in love and were living together. In 2011, DeKoe was deployed to Afghanistan. Before leaving, he and Kostura married in New York State (which allowed same-sex marriage). A week later, DeKoe began his deployment, which lasted for almost a year.

When DeKoe returned, the Army assigned him to work full-time in the Tennessee Army Reserve. Tennessee did not recognize their New York lawful marriage. So now they had to travel back and forth over state lines to fully live out their New York marriage. This was painfully ironic since DeKoe had served, and still served, his nation in defense of the Constitution but now must endure a substantial burden because Tennessee does not recognize his New York marriage.

The majority ruling does not go into the cases of the nine other plaintiffs but noted that each had their own experience and a story that made clear the significance and urgency of the same-sex marriage issue for them, especially given the democratic nature of our society and its respect for the sincere religious or religious-like convictions of all citizens.

Second, the majority ruling justices reviewed how marriage has been variously understood throughout the ages as well as today. They found that over millennia marriage had been understood from various perspectives: religious, spiritual, psychological, sociological, philosophical, historical, legal, and societal (that is, marriage as a social institution).

For example, marriages were (in some places still is) an arrangement made by the girl's parents with a man and often included her parents paying a dowry to her future husband. Among some cultural groups, polygamy, and at times even

---

2. The Supreme Court does not specify which of the couple was the state-recognized adopting parent.

polyandry, has been permitted. Often, too, upon marrying a girl lost many legal rights and was wholly subject to her husband.

The understanding of same-sex intimacy has also evolved. Not so long ago, such intimacy was targeted by the police and prohibited in military service, most governmental employment, and immigration. Today, changed, and still evolving, cultural and political attitudes have allowed LGBTQ persons to be more open about their sexual orientations.[3] (On these points, the justices cited a friend of the court brief filed by the Organization of American Historians.)

The ruling majority justices stated that they did not find it surprising that there are evolving understandings of marriage in nations where new generations of freedom have been occurring for years.

Third, the justices in the majority noted that at one time, in its 1952 *Diagnostic and Statistical Manual of Mental Disorders*, the American Psychiatric Association even considered same-sex orientation an illness. Only in recent years has this association recognized such orientations as a normal and immutable expression of human sexuality. (On this point, the court cited the American Psychiatric Association's friend of the court brief.)

Fourth, the court's majority even cited Confucius's teaching that marriage is at the foundation of government: for the first bond is marriage, the next children, and then family. Both religious and philosophical texts highlight the beauty of marriage. In brief, marriage is an essential societal institution.

---

3. Again, "L" refers to lesbians, "G" to gays, "B" to those with a double sexual orientation, "T" to those with the genitals of one sex, but the feelings of another, and "Q" to those who question or are not sure of what their real sexual orientation.

E. The Court's Ruling as Searching for a Mediating Middle Ground

The five justices felt a duty to do this careful societal justice analysis of marriage from the perspective of the individuals involved as well as from the perspective of marriage as a societal institution. They also felt that if their ruling were not to keep in mind these many perspectives, their legal argument might not be considered adequately sound.

In making their decision, the majority ruling justices spoke of marriage in glowing, panegyric-like terms. They wrote that:

> the annals of human history reveal the transcendent importance of marriage. The lifelong union of a man and a woman always has promised nobility and dignity to all persons, without regard to their station in life. Marriage is sacred to those who live by their religions and offers unique fulfillment to those who find meaning in the secular realm. Its dynamic allows two people to find a life that could not be found alone, for a marriage becomes greater than just the two persons.[4]

The five concurring justices also noted that it is not surprising that evolving understandings of marriage should occur in a nation where new generations of freedom have been occurring for generations. This dynamic evolution can also be seen in our nation's experience with the rights of gays and lesbian and other LGBTQ. Moreover, since the mid-twentieth century most Western nations have been gradually decriminalizing same-sex intimacy and have been increasingly recognizing the distinct dignity of same-sex couples' commitments and thereby excepting what was in their hearts.

Prior to that, such intimacy was targeted by the police and prohibited in military service, most government employment, and immigration. Today, changed cultural and political

---

4. Obergefell v. Hodges, 135 S. Ct. 2584 (2015). See https://www.supremecourt.gov/opinions/14pdf/14-556_3204.pdf.

attitudes have allowed LGBTQs to be more open and public about their lives and to raise and adopt children, and establish families. (On this point the court's ruling refers to a friend of the court brief presented by the Organization of American Historians.)

The concurring justices stressed that marriage has always fulfilled a central and most basic human need. Those who embrace it find it is essential to their most profound hopes and aspirations. So it is not surprising that traditional marriage has existed for millennia and has spanned all times, cultures, and civilizations. It transforms strangers into relatives and binds families and societies together.

F. The Court's Decision as a Compassionate, Respectful Search for and Finding a Nonjudgmental Mediating Middle Ground

In this context, the reader may want to keep in mind what the Catholic theologian/lawyer Cathleen Kaveny argued for in her book *Law's Virtues: Fostering Autonomy and Solidarity in American Society*. She referred to what the seventh-century historian, Isidore of Seville, had said: "Law should be virtuous, just, possible to nature, necessary, useful, according to the custom of the country, suitable to place and time, necessary, useful, clearly expressed, less by its obscurity it lead to misunderstanding."[5] Legal rulings and laws ought to be framed, not as if they were only for private benefit, but also for the common good.

The respondents, who represented the four states, argued that traditionally marriage has been seen as the gender differential union of two persons of the opposite sex. It should stay that way. If extended to include the union of two persons of the same sex, a timeless institution would be demeaned.

---

5. Kaveny, *Law's Virtues*, 271, 276n1. She found this quotation in Aquinas, *Summa Theologica*, II-II.95.3, where Aquinas cites Isidore of Seville.

The five concurring justices showed respect for that argument, recognizing that traditionally marriage has been seen as the union of two persons of opposite sex, and noted that it continues to be held by many reasonable, sincere persons of good faith both in the United States and throughout the world. They were emphatic they were not passing an ethical judgment of the morality of same-sex relations or questioning the good faith of those who hold traditional convictions about marriage.

However, they did reject the responders' claim that same-sex marriage would somehow demean the institution of marriage, especially in a nation that respects freedom of conscience and individual autonomy. They noted that the plaintiffs in this case acknowledge the timelessness of the traditional view; they only contend that our understanding of marriage should not end there. The plaintiffs were not demeaning marriage. On the contrary, they valued marriage so highly that they, too, wanted to share in this timeless institution and in the privileges and responsibilities that this institution entails and the human need for them. They see same-sex marriage as the only real path for doing so and feel a real urgency to share in it. They were asking that our nation's laws recognize their respect for marriage.

G. The Importance of Married Love for Society: an Encomium

The five majority justices ended their ruling with this compassionate, respectful encomium of married love for not only the couple but also for society as a whole:

> No union is more profound than marriage, for it embodies the highest ideals of love, fidelity, devotion, sacrifice, and family. In forming a marital union, two people become something greater than once they were. As some of the petitioners in these cases demonstrate, marriage embodies a love that may endure even past death. It would misunderstand these men and women to say they

disrespect the idea of marriage. Their plea is that they do respect it, respect it so deeply that they seek to find its fulfillment for themselves. Their hope is not to be condemned to live in loneliness, excluded from one of civilization's oldest institutions. They ask for equal dignity in the eyes of the law. The Constitution grants them this right.

The judgment of the Court of Appeals for the Sixth Circuit is reversed. It is so ordered.[6]

H. The Court's Decision as Compassionate, Respectful, and Nonjudgmental Interpretation of Law

In other words, the majority was very explicit that its ruling was not an ethical or religious judgment for or against same sex-marriage but only an effort to find a pragmatic, workable, and mediating middle ground decision on the issue that was in accord with the US Constitution as well as respectful of the liberty, dignity, and autonomy of the gays who sought a judicial ruling on the issue.

We have several times referred to Jesus' criticisms of some teachers of the Mosaic Law in his day for laying insupportable burdens on others without lifting a finger to ease it. Jesus' criticism was that they did not incorporate virtues such a compassion and understanding in their interpretations of Mosaic Law.

However, unlike the teachers of Mosaic Law whom Jesus criticized, the Supreme Court's ruling majority did indeed "lift a finger" by making use of the virtues of compassion and respect in interpreting the law of the land in favor of the plaintiffs while at the same time explicitly showing respect for those who disapproved of same-sex intimacy.

---

6. Obergefell v. Hodges, 135 S. Ct. 2584 (2015). See https://www.supremecourt.gov/opinions/14pdf/14-556_3204.pdf.

Bibliography

Abbott, Walter A., editor, *The Documents of Vatican II*. New York. Herder and Herder, 1966.
Adam, Margaret B. "Compassion." *Dictionary of Scripture and Ethics*, edited by Joel B. Green, 157–59. Grand Rapids: Baker Academics, 2011.
Alesina, Alberto, and Edward L. Glaeser. *Fighting Poverty in the US and Europe: A World of Difference*. Rodolfo Debenedetti Lectures. Oxford: Oxford University Press, 2004.
Allman, Anna. "Mommy and Daddy." *The New Republic*, January–February 2019.
American College of Obstetricians and Gynecologists. "ACOG Statement on Abortion Bans." https://www.acog.org/news/news-releases/2019/05/acog-statement-on-abortion-bans. Accessed February 10, 2020.
———. "Adolescents and Long-Acting Reversible Contraception: Implants and Intrauterine Devices." https://www.acog.org/clinical/clinical-guidance/committee-opinion/articles/2018/05/adolescents-and-long-acting-reversible-contraception-implants-and-intrauterine-devices. Assessed December 13, 2019.
Anderson, Gary A. "Adam." *The New Interpreter's Dictionary of the Bible: v. 1, A–C*, edited by Katharine Doob Sakenfeld, 1:48–50. Nashville: Abingdon, 2006.
Aquinas, Thomas. *Summa Theologica*. 3 vols. Translated by Fathers of the English Dominican Province. New York: Benziger, 1948.
Armstrong, Karen. *The Case for God: What Religion Really Means*. Anchor reprint edition. New York: Anchor, 2009.
———. *The Great Transformation*. Anchor Reprint edition. New York: Anchor, 2007.
———.*A History of God: The 4,000 Year Quest of Judaism, Christianity, and Islam*. Anchor reprint edition. New York: Anchor, 1994.
———. *Twelve Steps to a Compassionate Life*. Anchor reprint edition. New York: Anchor, 2011.

Bibliography

Artal-Mittelmark, Raul. "Stages of Development of the Fetus." https://www.merckmanuals.com/home/women-s-health-issues/normal-pregnancy/stages-of-development-of-the-fetus. Accessed November 10, 2019.

Beal, John P. and James A. Coriden, et al. *New Commentary on the Code of Canon Law*. New Jersey: Paulist, 2002.

Berger, Peter L. *The Sacred Canopy: Elements of a Sociological Theory of Religion*. New York: Anchor, 1990.

Berger, Peter L., and Thomas Luckmann. *The Social Construction of Reality: A Treatise in the Sociology of Knowledge*. New York: Anchor, 1966.

Bernardin, Joseph L., Cardinal. *The Seamless Garment: Writings on The Consistent Ethic of Life*. Maryknoll: Orbis, 2008.

Binney, James. *Astrophysics: A Very Short Introduction*. Oxford: Oxford University Press, 2016.

Boring, M. Eugene. "Matthew's Gospel." *The New Interpreter's Bible: General Articles on the New Testament, Matthew, Mark*, edited by Leander E. Keck, 8:241–51. Nashville: Abingdon, 1995.

Cahill, Lisa Sowle. "V. Roman Catholic Perspective." In *Bioethics: A–B*, edited by Bruce Jennings, 1:37–41. 4th ed. Farmington Hills, MI: Macmillan Reference USA, 2014.

Carr, David M. "Genesis." *The New Oxford Annotated Bible with Apocrypha: New Revised Standard Version*, edited by Marc Brettler et al., 7–17. 5th ed. Oxford: Oxford University Press, 2018.

Centers for Disease Control and Prevention. "Abortion Surveillance." https://www.cdc.gov/mmwr/volumes/68/ss/ss6811a1.htm. Assessed May 20, 2019.

———. "CDCs Abortion Surveillance System FAQs." https://www.cdc.gov/reproductivehealth/data_stats/abortion.htm. Accessed March 21, 2020.

———. "Contraception." https://www.cdc.gov/reproductivehealth/contraception/index.htm. Accessed March 21, 2020.

———. "Effectiveness of Family Planning Methods." https://www.cdc.gov/reproductivehealth/unintendedpregnancy/pdf/contraceptive_methods_508.pdf. Accessed March 25, 2019.

Coles, Peter. *Cosmology: A Very Short Introduction*. Oxford: Oxford University Press, 2016.

Coogan, Michael D. "In the Beginning: The Earliest History." *The Oxford History of the Biblical World*, edited by Michael D. Coogan, 3–24. Oxford: Oxford University Press, 1998.

Coogan, Michael D., ed. *The New Oxford Annotated Bible*. 3rd ed. Oxford: Oxford University Press, 1989.

Coriden, James A., et al., eds. *The Code of Canon Law: A Text and Commentary*. Mahwah, NJ: Paulist, 1985.

Cotter, Wendy. "Miracle." *The New Interpreter's Dictionary of the Bible: v. 5, R–Z*, edited by Katharine Doob Sakenfeld, 4:99–106. Nashville: Abingdon, 2009.

BIBLIOGRAPHY

Culpepper, R. Alan. "The Gospel of Luke." *The New Interpreter's Bible: Luke-John*, edited by Leander E. Keck, 9:3–490. Nashville: Abingdon, 1995.

Cuomo, Mario. "Religious Belief and Public Morality: A Catholic Governor's Perspective." http://archives.nd.edu/research/texts/cuomo.htm.

Donahue, John R. *The Gospel in Parable*. Philadelphia: Fortress, 1988.

———. "Parables, Use of." *Dictionary of Scripture and Ethics*, edited by Joel B. Green, 575–78. Grand Rapids: Baker Academic, 2011.

———. *Seek Justice that You May Live: Reflections and Resources on the Bible and Social Justice*. New York: Paulist, 2014.

Dworkin, Ronald. *Life's Dominion: An Argument about Abortion, Euthanasia, and Individual Freedom*. New York: Knopf, 1993.

———. *Religion without God*. Einstein Lectures. Cambridge: Harvard University Press, 2013.

Farley, Margaret A. *Just Love: A Framework for Christian Sexual Ethics*. New York: Continuum, 2006.

———. *Personal Commitments: Beginning, Keeping, Changing*. Rev. ed. Maryknoll: Orbis, 2013.

Flanagan, Caitlin. "The Things We Can't Face." *The Atlantic*, December 2019.

Fitzmyer, Joseph A. *The Gospel according to Luke I–IX: Introduction, Translation, and Notes*. Anchor Bible 28. New York: Doubleday, 1970.

———. *The Gospel according to Luke X–XXIV: Introduction, Translation, and Notes*. Anchor Bible 28A. New York: Doubleday, 1985.

Fosmoe, Margaret. "Mario Cuomo Speech at Notre Dame Focused on Abortion." *Southbend Tribune*, January 2, 2015. https://www.southbendtribune.com/news/local/mario-cuomo-speech-at-notre-dame-focused-on-abortion/article_e5f217f0-50e2-570b-9c98-83d8cf978bef.html. Accessed January 18, 2019.

Gaventa, Beverly R., and David L. Petersen. "General Articles on the Old Testament; Genesis; Exodus, Leviticus." *The New Interpreter's Bible: General Articles & Introduction, Commentary, & Reflections for Each Book of the Bible Including the Apocryphal/Deuterca*, edited by Leander E. Keck, 1:56–130. Nashville, Abingdon Press, 1995.

Grannan, Cydney. "What's the Difference Between Morality and Ethics?" https://www.britannica.com/story/whats-the-difference-between-morality-and-ethics. Assessed October, 2019.

Grisez, Germain. *Abortion, the Myths, the Realities, and the Arguments*. New York: Corpus, 1970.

Gustafson, James M., ed. *On Being Responsible: Issues in Personal Ethics*. New York: Harper Forum, 1968.

———. "A Protestant Ethical Approach." In *The Morality of Abortion: Legal and Historical Perspectives*, edited by John T. Noonan Jr., 101–21. Cambridge: Harvard University Press, 1970.

Hiebert, Theodore. "Create, To." *The New Interpreter's Dictionary of the Bible: v. 1, A–C*, edited by Katharine Doob Sakenfeld, 1:779–88. Nashville: Abingdon, 2006.

Bibliography

———. "Creation." *The New Interpreter's Dictionary of the Bible: v. 1, A–C*, edited by Katharine Doob Sakenfeld, 1:779–88. Nashville: Abingdon, 2006.

James, William. *Writings: 1902–1910*. The Library of America 38. New York: Library of America, 1988.

Jeremias, Joachim. *Parables of Jesus*. 2nd ed. New York: Prentice Hall, 1979.

Johnson, L. Syd M. "Ethical Perspectives." In *Bioethics*, edited by Bruce Jennings, 1:8–21. 4th ed. Farmington Hills, MI: Macmillan Reference USA, 2014.

Kaveny, Cathleen. *A Culture of Engagement: Law, Religion, and Morality*. Moral Traditions Series. Washington, DC: Georgetown University Press, 2016.

———. *Ethics at the Edges of Law: Christian Moralists and American Legal Thought*. Oxford: Oxford University Press, 2017.

———. *Law's Virtues: Fostering Autonomy and Solidarity in American Society*. Washington, DC: Georgetown University Press, 2016.

———. *Prophecy without Contempt: Religious Discourse in the Public Square*. Cambridge: Harvard University Press, 2016.

Mayo Clinic. "Amniocentesis." https://www.mayoclinic.org/tests-procedures/amniocentesis/about/pac-20392914. Accessed October 17, 2019.

———. "In-Vitro Fertilization (IVF)." https://www.mayoclinic.org/tests-procedures/in-vitro-fertilization/aboit/pac-20384716. Accessed October 17, 2019.

———. "Low Sperm Count." https://www.mayoclinic.org/diseases-conditions/low-sperm-count/symptoms-causes/syc-20374585. Accessed October 12, 2019.

Niebuhr, H. Richard. *The Responsible Self: An Essay in Christian Moral Philosophy: Introduction by James M. Gustafson*. Westminster: Harper & Row, 1963.

Obama, Michelle. *Becoming*. New York: Crown, 2018.

O'Brien, George Dennis. *The Church and Abortion: A Catholic Dissent*. Lanham: Rowman & Littlefield, 2010.

Orsy, Ladislas. "Canons and Commentary." *The Code of Canon Law: A Text and Commentary*, edited by James A. Coriden et al., 25–45. Mahwah, NJ: Paulist, 1985.

Patrizio, Pasquale, and Arthur L. Capla. "In Vitro Fertilization and Embryo Transfer." In *Bioethics: P–R*, edited by Bruce Jennings, 5:2769–75. 4th ed. Farmington Hills, MI: Macmillan Reference USA, 2014.

Paul VI, Pope. "Declaration of Religious Freedom." *The Documents of Vatican II*, edited by Walter M. Abbott, 672–97. New York: Herder & Herder, 1966.

Pew Research Center. "Public Opinion on Abortion, 1995–2019." https://www.pewforum.org/fact-sheet/public-opinion-on-abortion/. Accessed January, 22, 2020.

Pimpare, Stephen. *A People's History of Poverty in America*. New York: New Press, 2008.

BIBLIOGRAPHY

Pitard, Wayne T. "Before Israel: Syria-Palestine." In *The Oxford History of the Biblical World*, edited by Michael D. Coogan, 25–57. Oxford: Oxford University Press, 1998.

Planned Parenthood. "Emergency Contraception." https://www.plannedparenthood.org/learn/morning-after-pill-emergency-contraception. Accessed October 17, 2019.

Powderly, Kathleen E. "Social and Ethical Issues." In *Bioethics: P–R*, edited by Bruce Jennings, 5:1202–16. 4th ed. Farmington Hills, MI: Macmillan Reference USA, 2014.

Rahner, Karl. *Faith in a Wintry Season: Conversations and Interviews with Karl Rahner in the Last Years of His Life*. New York: Crossroad, 1990.

Ramsey, Paul. "Abortion: A Review Article." *The Thomist: A Speculative Quarterly Review* 37.1 (1973) 174–226.

Rogers, Carl R. *Client-Centered Therapy: Its Current Practice, Implications, and Theory*. Reprint, London: Constable, 2015.

Rosenfield, Allan, et al. "Medical Perspectives." In *Bioethics: A–B*, edited by Bruce Jennings, 1:1–7. 4th ed. Farmington Hills, MI: Macmillan Reference USA, 2014.

Sadler, T. W. *Langman's Medical Embryology*. 12th ed. Philadelphia: Lippincott, Williams & Wilkins, 2012.

Seow, C. L. "God, Names of." *The New Interpreter's Dictionary of the Bible*: v. 2, *D–H*, edited by Katherine Doob Sakenfeld, 2:588–95. Nashville, Abingdon, 2007.

Sher, Geoffrey, et al. *In Vitro Fertilization: The A.R.T of Making Babies (Assisted Reproductive Technology)*. 4th ed. New York: Skyhorse, 2013.

Smith, Mark. *The Early History of God: Yahweh and the Other Deities in Ancient Israel*. 2nd ed. Biblical Resource Series. Eerdmans, 2002.

Soards, Marian L. "The Gospel according to Luke, 1865–1916." *The New Oxford Annotated Bible with Apocrypha: New Revised Standard Version*, edited by Marc Brettler et al., 1865–916. 5th ed. Oxford: Oxford University Press, 2018.

Society for Assisted Reproductive Technology. "What Is SART?" https://www.sart.org/patients/what-is-sart. Assessed February 15, 2020.

Speiser, E. A. *Genesis: Introduction, Translation, and Notes*. Anchor Bible 1. Garden City: Doubleday, 1964.

Steinfels, Peter. "Can We Talk About Abortion? An Exchange," *Commonweal Magazine*, September 12, 2011. https://www.commonwealmagazine.org/can-we-talk-about-abortion. Accessed October 17, 2019.

Tatlok, Jason R. "Outcasts." *The New Interpreter's Dictionary of the Bible: v. 5, R–Z*, edited by Katharine Doob Sakenfeld, 4:347. Nashville: Abingdon, 2009.

Taylor, Charles. *A Secular Age*. Cambridge: Belknap, 2007.

Thomhave, Kalena. "Reproductive Rights At Risk With or Without Roe." *American Prospect*, Winter 2019. https://prospect.org/power/reproductive-rights-risk-without-roe/. Accessed October 17, 2019.

Bibliography

Throckmorton, Burton H., Jr. *Gospel Parallels: A Comparison of the Synoptic Gospels.* 5th ed. Nashville: Nelson, 1992.

Trible, Phyllis. "Eve." *The New Interpreter's Dictionary of the Bible: v. 2, D–H*, edited by Katherine Doob Sakenfeld, 2:358–60. Nashville: Abingdon, 2007.

Tyson, Neil deGrasse. *Astrophysics for People in a Hurry.* New York: Norton, 2017.

World Health Organization. "Preterm Birth." https://www.who.int/news-room/fact-sheets/detail/preterm-birth.

Index

abortion (1)
    case studies, 67. See also Gustafson, Kaveny.
    compassion 67
    conservative to liberal spectrum on abortion, 86–92
    direct, indirect, 62–63
    criminalization of. See legal observations.
    divisiveness and intractability of, 57–59
abortion, not the only option:
    examples of serious handicapped children who coped, 92–94.
    weighting degrees of sacredness, 85–87
abortion (2) five positions
    Catholic church (official), 62–66
    Dworkin's. 10, 61
    Gustafson, 70
    Kaveny, 73–76
    Rahner, Karl, 61, 66
Accountability and responsibility. See ethical norms
Armstrong, Karen, 11
    brief bio, 17
    compassion, 17–18

Cahill, Lisa Solle, 11, 62n12
compassion, 16–18, 74–75
    Armstrong on, 17–18
    Golden Rule, 18
conscience, freedom of, 64–66

dialogue, carrying on public policy, 3–5
discourse/dialogue, public policy discourse, 3–5, 115–16
double-effect principle, 63–64
Dworkin, Ronald, 11
    bio, 15n5
    his goal: Finding a mediating middle ground for discussion, 60–62, 78–80
    his liberal Paradigm, 88–92
    mini-conversations with eight other scholars, 11, 15
    position on abortion, 10
    sacredness. holy, Intrinsic value, sanctity, Dworkin on life's natural progression: from biological (*zoe*) to *lived* (bios) uniqueness of human life's sacredness, 80–81; Bernardin, 81n7 and our ironic responses to this sacredness. See also sacredness.

Index

epikeia (epiekeia), Aristotle, 65–66
ethics, author's model, four notions, 13–20
ethical choice between good or evil or worse, 13
ethics, author's model, four notions, 13–20
  (i) secular and pluralistic, 13, 15
  (ii) accountable/responsible, 13, 18
  (iii) religious/spiritual attitude or temperament, 15–16
  (vi) compassionate and respectful, 16, 19
do and don't and moral ideal models, 13, 20
ethical norms. 13–20
  absolute vs absolutely absolute, 19–20
  traditional do and don't and moral ideal models, 13–20s: See also societal justice analysis

family planning, 95–96
  contraception, 97–102
Farley, Margaret A., 11
Freedom, Religious, Vatican Declaration on, 65

Genesis, Book of, three Sesame-like stories
  creation of cosmos, Gen 1:1—2:3
  creation of cosmos, Gen 2:4–24
  ethical notions, 31, 34–35, 38–39
  origin of evil, Gen 3:1–24
God, personal and impersonal absolute mystery, 20–21
  driving force: awesome, and existentially as real as a sunset, 2, 15

timeless, spaceless, beyond all being, 21 *Religion without God* (Dworkin), 15
Gustafson, James M., 11
  case study, 67–75
  methodology, 70–72

human Reproduction. See reproduction and in-vitro fertilization

in-vitro fertilization (IVF), 107
  ethical issues, 110–11
  examples of some procedures, 109–10
  success rate, 110

James, William, 19–20
Jesus, criticizes teachers of Mosaic law, 23, 22, 123
John Paul, Pope, 76

Kaveny, Cathleen, 11
  Brief Bio, 72n24
  Case study, 7
  Also see legal observations.
knowledge, contextual, relative/relational nature of all human knowledge, 20–23

legal observations, 75–77
  criminalization of, 72–74
LGBTQ, 5, 10, 120
  defined, 5n2, 2–74
love and forgiveness, how they are related, 52
love, married, its importance for society and the individuals involved, 122–23
Luke, Gospel of, four sesame-like stories
  Good Samaritan parable (Lk 10:25–37)
  Prodigal Son parable (Lk 15:11–32)

Roman centurion sends for
Jesus (Lk, 7:1–10)
'A Sinful' Woman washes Jesus'
feet.

Mawhinney, John, 8
resume, 2, 5–7
author's ethical model and
methodology, 7–8, 12–20
See also societal justice analysis.
Mediating, middle ground, concessions and accommodations, 5
Messy, nitty-gritty world, 13, 21, 24–25
Moral, societal cultural mores, contextual, relative/relational nature of, 22–23
real-life examples, 24–24
mores, codes, societal, 22–23. See also ethical norms.

Niebuhr, H. Richard, 11, 12n1
nitty-gritty world, 24

O'Brien, George Dennis,11.

personhood, 193–106
genetic DNA individuality (Dworkin), 106
Vatican: Donum vitae (*Gift of Life*), 64
pluralistic. See secular/pluralist.
pragmatic, workable truth, 19
James, William, relative/relational nature of truth, 24
pro-life, pro-choice, 10, 58–59
prostitution

religious/spiritual attitude/temperament, 4–5
reproduction, human. See in-vitro fertilization (IVF), 107

responsible/accountable, 13

sacredness. the uniqueness of human life's sacredness, 80–81
our ironic responses to this sacredness, Bernardin, 81n7
sacredness, weighing the degrees of, 83. See also abortion, conservative to liberal spectrum
secular/pluralistic, 3–4
secular/secularity vs secularist/ secularism, 13–14
Sesame-like stories. See Genesis and Luke, Gospel of.
sexual orientations. See LGBTQ.
societal justice analysis, 7–8, 116–19
Supreme Court, US
Court ruling as an encomium of married love, 122–23
Court ruling as Jesus-like, compassionate, respectful non-judgmental and non-pharisaic interpretation of law
Court ruling as public policy discourse, 115–16
Court ruling as searching for and finding a mediating middle ground. 120
Court ruling as societal justice analysis, 116–18
Court's ruling on the essential importance of married love for both the couple and society

Taylor, Charles, (secular vs secularist), 11, 13
Truth and truth-value, scientific and moral: their contextual, relative/relational nature
See also pragmatic.